The Changing Southern Scene 1948-1981

The Changing Southern Scene 1948-1981

Michael Baker

LONDON

IAN ALLAN LTD

Previous page: Elmstead Woods with Class 71 No 71.008 heading a Hither Green-Dover freight in May 1974. *Brian Morrrison*

Below: Rebuilt 'West Country' Class No 34010 *Sidmouth* leaves Woking with a Waterloo-Bournemouth train in November 1963. *Brian Stephenson*

First published 1981

ISBN 0 7110 1090 0

Published by Ian Allan Ltd, Shepperton, Surrey; and printed by Ian Allan Printing Ltd at their works at Coombelands in Runnymede, England

Introduction

The trouble with having lived most of one's life on the Southern is that one rather takes it for granted. When I was a child a Southern suburban electric multiple-unit seemed as ordinary and as unexciting as a London tram, the milkman's horse, school dinners and the stained glass windows in our front door. In 1944 my father, who worked in the offices of NAAFI, was transferred to what had been in prewar days the Beacon Hotel on the cliffs at Bournemouth, and I had the first ride I could remember in a Southern Railway steam train. In wartime trains were too crowded for anyone who had hopes of obtaining a seat to waste time strolling up to look at the engine, and it was dark when we got to Bournemouth so I've no idea what pulled us. It could have been anything from a 'T9' to a 'Merchant Navy' although the odds are it was a 'Lord Nelson'. I recall one carriage had match-boarded sides which struck me as very peculiar and I assumed it was some form of temporary wartime arrangement. In reality it must have been one of the SECR Continental vehicles built in 1921. We didn't, as it happened, get a seat and had to stand in a guard's van which had not many hours previously been carrying fish; their memory certainly lingered on.

Back home in Thornton Heath in 1945 I moved schools and was initiated into the secrets of the Ian Allan *ABCs*. For 1s 6d (7½p) everything was revealed. The grimy black tank engines which shunted the yards at Thornton Heath, Selhurst and East and West Croydon now had an identity, and when one day returning from London a magnificent and immaculate locomotive in bright green livery with red-backed numberplates overtook our electric outside Clapham Junction I was able to recognise *South Foreland* as an 'H2' Atlantic. I even invested another 1s 6d in order to divine the mysteries of the hitherto despised Southern electrics and was much diverted to discover that the two-coach trains in which my father travelled to work between West Croydon and Wimbledon — he was now at NAAFI headquarters near Chessington Zoo — had once collected their power from overhead cables. The 'two trains' as we called them on account of their headcode and the number of coaches, were quite different internally from the rest of the suburban stock, with the sections of corridor and swinging dividing doors. The route they served was unique, too, being largely single-track and passing through a surprisingly rural part of suburbia once the Purley Way gas works had been negotiated.

Later on my father switched to the Streatham-Wimbledon line and on this the almost as ancient original LSWR multiple-units were frequently found. These too were distinctive, not merely for their pointed ends but also for the coupé compartment in their trailers. When the SR built 55 new suburban units in 1925 it gave the 25 intended for use on the Western Section pointed noses just like their LSWR predecessors although in every other respect they were identical to the flat-nosed Eastern Section ones. In later years it was discovered that flat and pointed units could work together on all three sections without any observable traumatic effects. The Southern continued to convert pre-Grouping steam stock into suburban multiple-units until 1937, although rather curiously a number of carriages built by the SECR immediately before the Amalgamation with an eye to their eventual conversion remained steam-hauled all their lives, the last of them ending their days on the Oxted line in the 1960s, but no more new stock appeared until 1942.

Pursuing our concern with noses and ends, those on the first Bulleid units, Nos 4101-10, were almost identical to his 2-HAL semi-fast sets of 1939 and had a clear Southern family likeness. Internally they were brutal, again like the HALs, and seated 460 passengers in six-a-side compartments, over a hundred more than in the original LSWR units.

After the war the Southern at last swung into production of new suburban multiple-units on a large scale, the first time this had happened in 37 years of electrified railways in South London. The sloping cab roofs of the first Bulleid units had gone and internally they allowed passengers a little more room. Some had a semi-saloon trailer and this civilised arrangement was soon extended to the motorcoaches, and three saloons and one compartment coach became the standard 4-SUB formation. Although there were less seats there was more standing room and more space to move about in and, incidentally, less chance of being set upon by vandals, robbers, and sex and religious maniacs. Compartment carriages almost invite vandalism as was only too obvious in the early 1970s in the Southern-type Euston and Broad Street emus. Not that vandalism is as peculiar to our age as

the prophets of doom would have us believe; Hamilton Ellis for example cites instances of deliberate damage to carriages going back to the earliest days of rail travel.

The 4-SUBs were succeeded by the 4-EPBs, in many respects identical, and, despite emerging three years after Nationalisation, pure Southern Railway. However there were several important innovations, chief of these being the use of electropneumatic braking, hence the designation 4-EPB. It was a time when the Southern was giving considerable thought to the improvement of rush-hour services, and better acceleration and deceleration would allow more trains to be fitted into the timetable.

An even bolder, although in the event, less successful innovation was the celebrated double-deck train of 1949. Delays in getting in and out offset its increased capacity and in 1954 a less exciting but more practical solution appeared in the form of two-car 2-EPB units, thus enabling 10-coach trains to be run during the rush-hour. Before their introduction many stations on the Eastern Section had their platforms lengthened and the 10-coach trains were restricted to this part of the system. The 2-EPBs first brought the BR Standard design and a new, 63ft 11$\frac{1}{2}$in, length to the Southern, but the Southern Railway one was far from dead. When more 2-EPBs and semi-fast 2-HAPs came out in 1958-9 on old 2-NOL underframes their 62ft 6in-long bodies reverted to Bulleid contours.

The long-distance emus, except for the 2-NOLS, were all built new. I used to watch them with some awe thunder along between Norbury and Thornton Heath, travelling at an immense rate compared to the sedate suburban stopping trains, the rear driver's cab swaying and bouncing as that distinctive ringing clatter of the bogie and shoes receded, leaving a flurry of dust and scraps of paper dancing along the track behind. The motorcoaches of the 6-PUL and 6-PAN units were rather like elegant tanks. For more than 30 years they thumped their 57 tons up and down the Brighton line, and although their cushions were a good deal deeper and their appointments generally rather more luxurious than those of the 4-CIGs and 4-BIGs which replaced them, they had a well deserved reputation for rough riding and their British Rail successors when they arrived in the mid-1960s seemed astonishingly well-behaved by contrast. The 4-CORs, the 4-RESs and the 4-BUFs were better and

3H unit No 1120 pulls out of Hailsham for Eastbourne just before closure in 1968.

the 4-CORs survived into the 1970s to become the last of all the Southern Railway main line emus.

The 2-BILs were perhaps the most handsome. Even in their final years, although a trifle shabby, their restrained, varnished wood interiors and comfortable cushions remained inviting. Their successors, the 2-HALs, had never been that. Their grey-painted interiors were uncomfortably reminiscent of a barracks, the motorcoaches had neither corridors nor lavatories and their windows were unnecessarily small. Perhaps they rode as well as the BILs but their other disabilities combined to suggest that they did not. The best of them were the eight postwar ones.

The most famous Southern multiple-units were, of course, the 15 Pullmans used on the 'Brighton Belle' for 40 years and all now preserved, but my favourites were the 4-LAVs. Unspectacular and reliable, well-proportioned and rather better riding than their 6-PUL and 6-PAN contemporaries, they seemed ageless. They wore green livery all their lives; just one, No 2954, acquired all-yellow ends. That they should ever be replaced seemed unthinkable but of course time caught up with them. The first was withdrawn in 1967 and two years later the 4-VEPs had replaced them all.

I make no apology for dwelling at some length on the Southern emus. They, after all, have operated the most intensive and extensive electric suburban railway system in the world for 50 years; and perhaps, also, I owe it to them for having taken them so much for granted in my youth. Elsewhere electric trains might have been rather unusual and avant garde but in the South London suburbs when I was growing up they were as common as plane trees and yellow-grey brick churches.

Southern steam engines and locomotive-hauled carriages fall fairly neatly into four groups, pre-1923, Maunsell, Bulleid, and BR Standard. Admittedly Maunsell began his career at Ashford 10 years before the Southern Railway came into existence, and Bulleid's Pacifics after rebuilding were a mixture of his and BR practice, but with these exceptions the distinctions are reasonably clear cut. In 1948 express passenger, goods, and tank engines from the London & South Western, London Brighton & South Coast, and South Eastern & Chatham companies all existed in considerable numbers, which wasn't something you could say of the London & North Western, for example. And Brighton Atlantics, Urie 'N15s', and South Eastern 'Ls', 'D1s' and 'E1s' went on hauling express trains well into the 1950s, alongside Bulleid Pacifics, the most modern passenger locomotives in Britain.

Unlike the rest of the Big Four the Southern Railway never built any suburban tank engines — the short-lived 'River' 2-6-4Ts were strictly for express traffic — which was not surprising given the Southern's drive for electrification. For all that, immediately after Nationalisation Brighton Works embarked on an ambitious programme of first LMS

Below: Class 33 No 6511 arrives at Basingstoke with a test train consisting of new Bournemouth line electric stock in September 1966. *M. Pope*

and then BR Standard 2-6-4Ts. One-time suburban tanks from the 19th century and the Edwardian era were to be found on rural and semi-rural branches from Kent to Cornwall, usually in charge of equally ancient carriages.

The Southern was a great line for 4-4-0s. Drummond 'T9s' and Wainwright/Maunsell 'Ls', 'D1s' and 'E1s' still had charge of London expresses as late as 1961, whilst the 'Schools' were, of course, the last and most powerful of the type in Europe, outside Ireland. In the 1940s and for most of the 1950s they were almost exclusively Eastern Section engines, but after the first stage of the South Eastern main line electrification in 1959 they were to be found at Brighton, Reading, Salisbury, Bournemouth and elsewhere in the West. The last active Atlantics in Britain were to be found on the Brighton line, whilst the oldest locomotives of all were the Stroudley 'Terriers', 10 of which have been preserved.

The Hastings line diesel-electric multiple-units replaced the once familiar SEC birdcage sets and three years later electrification on much of the rest of the Eastern Section saw the beginning of the end of Maunsell main line stock. The year 1962 was a real watershed for in that year the 'Nelsons', Arthurs' and 'Schools' all disappeared and after that the remaining steam-operated main line, to Bournemouth and Weymouth, lost much of its interest, the rebuilt Bulleid Pacifics which predominated from then not being in my opinion a particularly good-looking design. Along with them were Bulleid design carriages. These lasted as long as steam on the Southern. Even after the end in the summer of 1967 a handful of Bulleid carriages found employment in the north-east and one has been preserved on the Keighley & Worth Valley Railway.

I have said elsewhere that the rebuilt Bulleid Pacifics are not everyone's idea of a handsome locomotive. There is certainly something not quite right about the shape of the smokebox door, and the whole front end relationship of smokebox front, smoke deflectors and framing. And in their last years on the Bournemouth line they were often grubby and neglected, which didn't help. But it has to be admitted that the restored No 34016, *Bodmin*, with her immaculate Brunswick green paintwork, red-backed nameplates, varnished wood cab window framing and sparkling motion and pipework, is a stirring sight.

Although the Mid-Hants was a latecomer to the preservation scene it has achieved a great deal in a very short time and is now one of the principal agencies in the restoration of Southern rolling stock.

Since 1967 the only class of locomotive allocated to the non-electric lines of the Southern has been the Crompton Class 33, an efficient and hard-working but scarcely exciting design. However there have been many regular visitors, ranging from the 'Warships' and the Class 50s on the Exeter line to Class 47s which are seen all over the Southern. But if it's variety you're after then today it is to be found where the electrics hold sway.

Below: Class 71 No E5015 arrives at Dover Marine with the 'Golden Arrow' in June 1961. *BR*

Above: No 30586, one of the prehistoric Beattie '0298' class 2-4-0Ts of the 1870s, removes a van from the rear of the overnight train from Waterloo at Wadebridge on 10 May 1958. Designed for London suburban work, all but three of the class had been withdrawn before the end of the 19th century. The three survivors worked another 60 years on the Wadebridge to Wenford mineral line and when not on this duty filled in on light work around Wadebridge. No 30586 was the unlucky one of the three, the two others being preserved, at Quainton Road and on the Dart Valley. Wadebridge was almost as far west as you could go on the Southern; Padstow, five miles away, being Waterloo's most westerly outpost. *Brian Morrison*

Right: Gunnislake is now the most westerly limit of what was once Southern territory, although for well over a decade it has been part of the Western Region. Originally an intermediate station on the Callington branch which left the Plymouth-Exeter main line at Bere Alston, Gunnislake is now the terminus of a diesel multiple-unit service from Plymouth. A two-car unit stands ready to return back along the Cornwall/Devon border to Plymouth in September, 1969. *Michael Baker, as are all uncredited photographs*

Bottom right: The railway history of the West Country is essentially that of a rivalry between the LSWR and the Great Western, a rivalry which continued beyond the Grouping and into the days of Dr Beeching, who more or less decided the issue in favour of the Western.

The LSWR main line north of Bere Alston was closed in 1968 and since then the old Great Western main line has had a monopoly of traffic between Cornwall, Plymouth and London. But in May 1961 when this picture was taken it was still possible to set out from Plymouth for Waterloo in charge of one of Drummond's 'T9' 4-4-0s of 1899. No 30709 with a characteristic eight-wheel watercart tender climbs out of Bere Alston with the 10.02 to Waterloo. In the right background is the viaduct carrying the Callington branch over the Tamar and into Cornwall. *S. C. Nash*

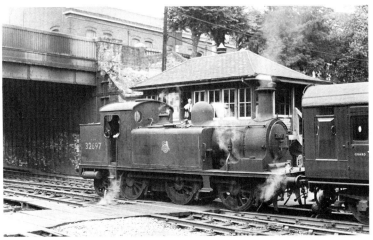

Above: The Meldon-Exeter section of the former LSWR main line survives, now also part of the Western Region as this picture with the GWR type signals and the Class 25 makes very clear. The setting is Crediton, the date May 1979. The driver is handing over the staff for what is now the single-track section to Okehampton and Meldon. Long, long ago the Exeter & Crediton Railway was a broad gauge concern, so its return to the Western fold is not entirely inappropriate. But the signalbox is typically South Western, and later that morning the Southern presence was reinforced by the arrival of the 10.57 dmu from Exmouth towing a Southern Railway-built four-wheel general utility van.

Centre left: A feature of the scene at Exeter Central in steam days was the bankers which heaved trains up the 1 in 37 from the Western station at St Davids. The best known were the 'E1R' 0-6-2Ts, Maunsell rebuilds of Stroudley 'E1' 0-6-0Ts built by the LBSCR between 1874 and 1884. The 83-year old No 32697, the last survivor, at the rear of a Waterloo express in the summer of 1959, a few weeks before withdrawal. *Stanley Creer*

Bottom left: A St Davids-Exmouth dmu approaches Exeter Central in May 1979.

11

Above: Although Yeovil possesses two stations neither is very conveniently situated, Pen Mill on the Weymouth-Westbury line being on the eastern edge of the town whilst Yeovil Junction on the Exeter-Salisbury line is at the end of a winding country lane. The joint GW/LSW Town station was much handier but unfortunately was served by a little-used branch line. From left to right in this view of Yeovil Town shed on 20 September 1964 are 'Warship' No D817 *Foxhound*, a Swindon built Cross Country dmu, the pioneer Standard Class 4 4-6-0 No 75000, a Maunsell 'U' class 2-6-0 lurking behind the water column and more Standard '4' 4-6-0s. The rapid expansion of Yeovil could not save the Town station and yard, which closed in 1967, and the site is now a car park. *Tony Trood*

Right: Towards the end of 1979 the long-promised Class 50 'Warships' began to appear regularly on the Waterloo-Exeter line as HST workings increased on the WR's West of England main line. By the beginning of 1980, Class 50s had replaced the '33s' on the 06.15 and 07.45 up trains and the 11.00 and 13.00 down workings, reviving memories of the Class 42/43 diesel hydraulics with their warship names. On 31 January 1980 No 50.050 *Fearless* stands at Yeovil Junction with the 13.00 Waterloo-Exeter.

Above left: When Dr Beeching decided that there was no need for two main lines to the West, the Southern's was allowed to remain as far as Exeter but as a very second rate affair. Expresses disappeared, as did most of the stations and those that remained were served by semi-fasts running at two-hourly intervals. Perhaps the most controversial feature of this rationalisation was the singling of much of the line, which was no aid to good timekeeping. Chard Junction was one of the stations closed but the buildings and platform remained on the up side and the signalbox is still in use as trains cross here. In May 1979 the 17.06 Exeter to Yeovil Junction waits opposite the milk depot for the road which is occupied by the late running 15.00 from Waterloo. Through trains are always locomotive-hauled but the very limited number of Exeter-Honiton-Yeovil Junction- Salisbury ones are often the province of Exeter-based dmus. Milk traffic today, as it always has been, is a feature of the West Country railway scene.

Above: At Salisbury the Waterloo-Exeter line connects with the important Bristol- Southampton cross-country line. In pre- nationalisation days this latter belonged to the Great Western west of Salisbury but it is now Southern property as far as Westbury. Conversely the old Southern main line is Western property west of Wilton junction where the Bristol and Exeter lines converge. Western locomotives have always been familiar at Salisbury and in this view of the shed taken on 1 July 1959 'King Arthur' Nos 30449 *Sir Torre* and 30774 *Sir Gaheris* stand alongside Great Western Mogul No 7332 and a 'County' 4-6-0.

Right: 'King Arthur' No 30786 *Sir Lionel* pulls out of Salisbury with the 16.05 all stations to Woking and then semi-fast to Waterloo, a typical duty for the class in its later days. By this date, 1 July 1959, scrapping of the 30 'Scotch Arthurs', as those built by North British in Glasgow were always known, had begun. *Sir Lionel* was a Nine Elms engine, one of the four Western Section sheds to which the class was allocated, the others being Basingstoke, Bournemouth and Salisbury. No 30786 was withdrawn the following month.

Above right: Twenty years later on 15 June 1979, No 31.421 passes the site of the shed — now a rich breeding ground for wild flowers, shrubs and small trees — with the 14.07 Portsmouth Harbour to Bristol, and close to the spot where Constable painted the cathedral which fills the background. The six-coach train is typical of formations used on this service with a full brake in the middle, a solitary Mk IIb, and stock with Western, Eastern and Midland prefixes.

Centre right: Following the withdrawal of the 'Warships', which had worked the Waterloo-Exeter trains since the rationalisation of the route in 1965, the less powerful but more reliable Crompton/BRCW Class 33s took over. The 11.00 down train is seen approaching Salisbury Tunnel junction on 28 October 1979. Although by this date some of the trains were composed of Mk IIb, stock most of the carriages provided by the Western Region for the service were elderly Mk Is dating back to steam days.

Below: No 10201, the first of Bulleid's English Electric 1Co-Co1 1,750hp diesel-electrics leaves Salisbury with the 13.00 Waterloo to Plymouth express on 2 July 1954. Built in 1951, Nos 10201/2 and the similar but more powerful No 10203 of 1954 were, like the pioneer LMS twins, precursors of the 'Peaks' and the Class 40s.
Brian Morrison

Above: The end of the Weymouth junction to Portland branch came on 27 March 1965. LMS Class 2 2-6-2T No 41324 passes the site of Rodwell station in western Weymouth with the last train on a line which had once been a lifeline linking the Prison, the Naval Base and the people of the bleak island of stone with the mainland. Until late 1979 the rails still remained across the road at the north end of the station; the trackbed has been regrassed to form a popular walk — although the intention is that it should eventually form part of a new road to Portland — and a rusty padlock long continued to secure the gate locked after the last ordinary passenger train departed. *Tony Trood*

Below: In the last days of steam, enthusiasts' specials took many classes far from their usual haunts. One of the more remarkable sights was that of a Gresley 'A4' at Weymouth. No 60024 *Kingfisher* gathers speed past Weymouth shed on 25 March 1966 with a returning LCGB Special to Waterloo. A housing estate now stands on the site of the shed. *Tony Trood*

Top: The Channel Islands boat train was the last on British Rail regularly to sport carriage destination boards, thus affording the unique spectacle of a blue and grey Mk II coach so equipped. Nineteen Mk II firsts were delivered in green livery to the Southern in 1963 and these long remained the only examples of their type in the Region, everything else being variations on the Mk I theme. The Mk IIs are to be found on the Weymouth and Southampton boat trains and on Oxted line rush hour services.

Above: The last day of steam working on the Weymouth boat trains was 8 July 1967. No 35023, minus her *Holland-Afrika* nameplates, approaches Radipole Halt, the first station out of Weymouth at the foot of the long climb through the Downs to the summit at Bincombe Tunnel. Enthusiasts lean out of the first coach; the Great Western pagoda shelters on the platforms at Radipole survived for another 10 years and were among the last in use. They were replaced by a pair of less distinctive but more salubrious 'Clasp' structures. *Tony Trood*

Above: One of the sights of Weymouth is the Channel Islands boat train, trundling along the streets amongst the road traffic and the holidaymakers on its way to the Quay. Until 1960 the service ran to and from Paddington by way of Yeovil and the West of England main line, but in that year it was transferred to Waterloo and since then its London terminus has been Waterloo. After the demise of the pannier tanks which hauled it between the Quay and Weymouth junction it was put in the charge of Class 03 diesel shunters. Subsequently it was discovered that Class 33s could negotiate the sharp curves around the edge of the Harbour and here, in June 1979, No 33.112, with yellow flashing lamp and preceded by two railmen with flags, eases her way between the boats and parked cars.

Centre left: On a wet November day in 1979 a '33' entertains a suitably clad family as she runs round her train at the Quay station with the Sealink ferry *Maid of Kent* in the background, laid up for the winter.

Bottom left: Ornate gaslamps at Weymouth Town in February 1974, just before they succumbed to electricity. Elegant relics, their survival into the 1970s was symptomatic of the run-down state of the station, a wooden structure built by the Great Western, long served by Southern and Western trains and now the sole property of the Southern Region.

17

Above: Dorchester South on 27 August 1954. No 30739, *King Leodegrance*, one of the original LSW-built Urie 'N15' 4-6-0s later incorporated into Maunsell's 'King Arthur' class, is about to depart with the 14.20 Weymouth to Andover Junction. The latter part of its roundabout route, between Kimbridge junction on the Romsey-Salisbury line and Andover, has been long since abandoned. *King Leodegrance* was scrapped in 1956, and in 1971 a platform was built alongside the up main line at Dorchester thus at last relieving eastbound trains of the need to reverse into the station as *King Leodegrance* had just done. The curious original layout of Dorchester South was the result of the line being part of a projected route to the West which in the event was never built. Instead the LSW did a sharp left turn, joined up with the GW, and retreated through the Downs to Weymouth. The Great Western station, Dorchester West, now reduced to the status of an unstaffed halt, is situated at the end of the road directly above the station sign.
R. C. Riley

Centre right: Between Morton and Dorchester, February 1978. During the almost unprecedented snows in the winter of 1978 Dorchester's only link with the outside world for several days was the railway. The driver of a '33' in the charge of a 4-TC Class 491 unit from Bournemouth telephones for permission to pass a signal at red protecting a level crossing, the barriers of which are buried in a snowdrift.

Bottom right: There could hardly be a greater contrast than with this scene six months later as a '33' thunders across the Lulworth road near East Stoke with the 13.35 Waterloo to Weymouth on a warm afternoon in early September 1978. With the end of steam in the summer of 1967 an hourly service of diesel-hauled trains took over — diesel hauled, that is, west of Bournemouth. Between there and Waterloo the 4-TC unit (two units in summer and on Friday evenings all the year round) couples with a 2,920hp 4-REP (Class 430) and works as an express usually stopping only at Southampton.

18

Top: Wareham station, 4 May 1966. The now preserved rebuilt 'Merchant Navy' No 35028, *Clan Line*, with the 16.35 Waterloo-Weymouth train stands alongside Standard 2-6-4T No 80065 at the head of the connecting 19.28 Swanage branch train. For many years a preserve of 'M7s' and auto trains, the Swanage branch survived the end of steam and from 1967 was worked by demus until succumbing in January 1972.   *Tony Trood*

Above: Summertime saw through trains between Swanage and London, the Midlands and the North of England. The driver applies a drop more lubrication to an already excessively oily rebuilt Light Pacific, No 34004, *Yeovil*, before setting off from Swanage with the 11.34 for Waterloo on 20 September 1964.   *Tony Trood*

Above: When the remainder of the line was closed, some two miles of the Swanage branch from Worgret junction to Furzebrook were kept open and a goods train has continued to run along it to the Furzebrook clay works each weekday. But something rather remarkable was going to happen to this insignificant little stretch of branchline. It had been known for some time that there were certain oil deposits beneath the Isle of Purbeck but when exploration was stepped up in the mid-1970s it quickly became obvious that there was a great deal more beneath the beautiful heathland around the shores of Poole Harbour and out into the Channel beyond Swanage than had ever been suspected. A terminal was erected on the opposite side of the line to the clay works at Furzebrook and the first trainload of oil departed just before Christmas 1978. In November 1979 a Class 47 runs round its train of 10 empty 100-ton tankers prior to reversing them into the Furzebrook terminal.

Below: A day worth waiting for, 5 August 1979, the first day of public operation on the restored Swanage Railway. Even before closure local — and not so local — residents and enthusiasts were planning to restore the Swanage branch. Nevertheless the track was removed for the greater part of its length but by August 1979 a few hundred yards had been relaid north from the goods shed at Swanage and when the season ended a month later 1,603 passengers had been carried in a partly restored Bulleid brake third hauled by a small four-wheel diesel. It was a modest beginning, but the line owns a number of steam locomotives in varying states of restoration plus other rolling stock and even if it reopens only as far as Corfe Castle, with such a tourist attraction on its route it must surely succeed.

Top: From its beginnings in the early 19th century Bournemouth has always considered itself a superior sort of place and unlike almost all other seaside towns was not very anxious to encourage the railway and the hordes of hoi polloi it might bring with it. Consequently neither the misnamed Central nor the West stations were close either to the town centre or the sea, unlike nearby Poole where the station is not only slap bang in the middle of the town but is also right beside the harbour. If anything Bournemouth West was slightly handier than the Central station, but it was a terminus which didn't facilitate through working and its site is now occupied by the Bournemouth Ring Road, although the adjacent carriage sheds remain. In this scene at Bournemouth West on a sunny Sunday evening in April 1965 a Hampshire demu, Class 205 No 1132, pulls out as empty stock to Basingstoke beside a 4-TC in original blue livery; a rebuilt Light Pacific No 34089, *602 Squadron* waits to leave with the 19.25 to Waterloo, and a Crompton Class 33, No D6553, stands at the head of the through 19.32 Brighton train. *Tony Trood*

Above: Somerset & Dorset trains normally used Bournemouth West but this special is leaving the south end of the Central station on 7 June 1964. It is in the charge of ex-LMS '4F' 0-6-0 No 44568 and one of the unique Derby-built 2-8-0s, No 53807, the most characteristic of all S&D locomotives. The joint Southern/Midland ownership of the Somerset & Dorset and its total absence of diesels ensured some fascinating combinations of motive power and coaching stock right until the end, which came on 7 March 1966. Tank engines, however, were rare although one day in 1944 when we were living near Bournemouth West my father came home from work at lunchtime and reported the presence of a large tank engine in the station. It is unlikely to have been a big Maunsell or Urie tank and was probably a Fowler or Stanier 2-6-4T strayed south of Birmingham over the S&D. *Tony Trood*

Above: At Bournemouth today diesel traction is exchanged for electric. Until their demise the '71s' were the usual motive power for the boat trains. They have been succeeded by the '73s' and here No 73.123 waits in the bay platform for the up train in May 1979 while an intending passenger studies the *Daily Telegraph,* a very popular paper in Bournemouth.

Above right: The north end of Bournemouth station, June 1979, and a 4-REP Class 430 which has just arrived from Waterloo. These 2,920hp units power all the London-Bournemouth expresses. Their riding, like most BR designed emus is much better than their SR predecessors, except when they are due for works, when it deteriorates to rival the old 6-PULs and PANs. But generally these units are very dated when compared even with the Mark IIa stock which runs into Bournemouth on inter-Regional trains from the Midlands and the north, let alone the air-conditioned stock found on much of the rest of the Inter-City network.

Right: The south end of Bournemouth station (the Central has been long dropped) in September 1979. On the left are two of the 4-VEP Class 423 units introduced on semi-fast and stopping services in 1967, and on the right No 33.119 with the Channel Islands boat train.

Above: With the exception of the *Queen Elizabeth II* during the summer months, regular ocean travel to and from Southampton has virtually ceased, leaving only the cruise liners which call perhaps two or three times a month. In December 1979 a Class 33 pulls out from the Western Docks with a Waterloo train conveying passengers from the *Canberra* which has just arrived from a Mediterranean cruise and is about to go into dry dock for overhaul.

Centre right: Southampton Central, January 1967. A Standard Class 4 2-6-0 pulls out on a local goods under the famous gantry at the south end of the station. In the background, in the Western Docks, is the *Queen Mary*, destined to survive the end of steam on the Southern by a few months. Note the typical Southern reinforced concrete lamp-posts, the 12-car stop signs and the third rail for the impending electrification.

Bottom right: One of the wartime American-built USA 0-6-0Ts, No 30069, shunts in the Western Docks in front of the impressive Solent flour mills. Used extensively in the Docks in the latter days of steam four of these fascinating engines have been preserved. *Stanley Creer*

Above: Semaphore signals survived in profusion in the Southampton area well into the electric area. Of the many gantries the two most impressive were at the south end of what used to be Southampton Central, now simply Southampton, and this one at St Denys where the Waterloo and Portsmouth lines diverge. Both remained in use in the summer of 1980 but by then their days were numbered. Electric colour lights replaced semaphores on the Portsmouth line beyond St Denys in the spring of that year and renewal work continued steadily towards the city centre. Portsmouth line Class 205 demus pass at St Denys 25 March 1980.

Below: Until the early 1960s Ocean Liner expresses were commonplace on the Waterloo-Southampton line, conveying passengers, sometimes very glamorous ones, film stars, statesmen and the like to and from a host of equally glamorous ocean giants serving the Five Continents. On 2 June 1959 No 30856, *Lord St Vincent*, rolls a typical boat express through Wandsworth Cutting. The eighth vehicle is an old Pullman repainted in green livery and used as a restaurant car.

Left: 4-VEP Class 423 unit No 7802 approaches Lymington junction on a Waterloo-Lymington Pier working in September 1978. The line on the right is a new link under construction between Brockenhurst and the branch, opened some weeks later and enabling Brockenhurst-Lymington trains to keep clear of the main line. Through trains to and from Waterloo run only on summer Saturdays, the branch normally being worked at this period by a 2-SAP (Class 418) unit. The VEPs are marginally more comfortable but their thin cushions, three-plus-two seating layout and two lavatories per unit make them highly unsuitable for journeys of any length, despite which they are regularly so employed all over the electrified lines of the Southern Region.

Below: Class 4 2-6-0 No 76006 backs out of Portsmouth Harbour station on 10 August 1963 after bringing in empty stock. The typical Southern Railway-built brick and concrete signalbox was replaced in the 1970s. *Stanley Creer*

Right: The Isle of Wight railways have always had a special attraction, time seemingly passing them by. On a lovely June day in 1952 LSWR-built '02' 0-4-4T No W23, *Totland*, wheels a train of ex-SEC and LBSC carriages through typical Island scenery on a Ventnor-Ryde working. *Brian Morrison*

Below right: All the '02s' (indeed all the Island engines) carried names. No 14, *Fishbourne*, stands at Ryde Esplanade on 19 August 1966. In this view the enlarged bunker, fitted in the Island workshops at Ryde, can be clearly seen, as can the lack of moulding on the ex-LBSC brake second, another example of the ingenious Island engineers' make do and mend. *Tony Trood*

Left: The '02s' monopolised passenger traffic from the late 1920s until the end of steam on the last day of December 1966. But four LBSC Stroudley 'E1' 0-6-0Ts lasted into BR days on the limited goods workings and No 4 *Wroxall* (Island engines never bore smokebox number plates) stands in the yard at Newport in May 1955. Although Newport is the Island capital its rail services did not survive the end of steam.

Below: Electrification hardly meant modernisation. Because of clearance problems it was not possible to use full-size stock and so the unfortunate Islanders (and the holidaymakers who ensured the survival of the Ryde-Shanklin line when all else had gone) had 11 ancient ex-London Transport tube trains dumped on them. No 042, one of the 4-VEC, Class 485, four-car units, stands outside St Johns works, Ryde in September 1979. These ancient relics are quite dreadful, with dark, gloomy interiors and very inferior riding qualities.

Right: The Isle of Wight Steam Railway has preserved 1¾ miles of the Newport-Ryde line and has its headquarters at Haven Street. It has three ex-SEC and three ex-LBSC carriages in working order, the oldest of the latter being No 2416, a rebuilt third turned out at Lancing in 1916, and restored to Southern Railway malachite green livery. The smoking signs, typical of SR practice, survive in a number of the windows.

Above: The railway has a fine 'O2', carefully restored to working condition, but the most gorgeous spectacle on view at Haven Street in September 1979 was 'Terrier' No W8, *Freshwater,* newly arrived from Hayling Island and painted in the beautiful Southern Railway olive green with black and white lining of the inter-war period.

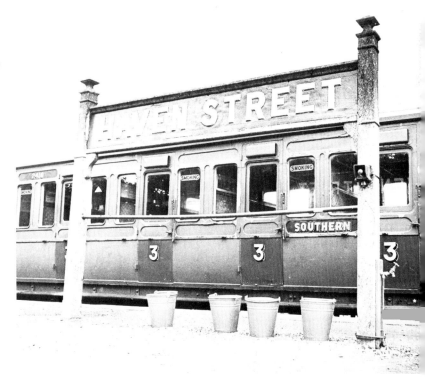

Top: Then, as now, Western Region locomotives regularly worked through trains from the north and the Midlands over Southern metals. No 4964, *Rodwell Hall*, hurries the 08.35 Newcastle-Bournemouth West past Worting junction on 22 May 1961.

Above: A 'Hymek' diesel-hydraulic in charge of a Bristol-Portsmouth Harbour train approaches Redbridge at the head of Southampton Water in November 1968. The fifth coach is a buffet car and the train carries waistlevel destination boards, symbols of a prestige which was soon to vanish from this service. In the early 1970s the Southern took over from the Western and could provide nothing better than uncomfortable demus. But by the later 1970s things had looked up, with the return of locomotive-hauled stock, in the charge of Western Class 31s, replaced in the summer of 1980 by Southern '33s', and, once in a while, a '47'; there was also a considerable speeding up, the fastest trains stopping only at Bath and Salisbury on the 1hr 44min journey from Bristol to Southampton.

Above: For a time in the 1950s all five pioneer main line diesels, the three Bulleid 1Co-Co1s and the two Derby-built Co-Cos, were at work on the Western Section. The first of them all, No 10000, built by the LMS and English Electric at Derby in 1947, is seen between Shawford and Eastleigh with the down 'Royal Wessex' on 2 July 1954. If ever a diesel deserved preservation this, the daddy of them all, was surely the one. *Brian Morrison*

Below: Southampton has developed into a container terminal of great importance. No 47.074 gathers speed through Eastleigh with a Freightliner train for Ripple Lane, Dagenham. Although the Southern has no regular allocation of '47s', they are a familiar sight on inter-Regional freight and passenger workings and are particularly common around Eastleigh.

Above left: The Hayling Island branch was a favourite haunt of the astonishingly long-lived Stroudley 'Terriers'. Nos 32661 and 32677 double-head an empty stock train at Farlington junction, where the branch diverged from the Portsmouth-Brighton coast line, on 17 July 1955. The Stanier corridor ahead of the three ex-LSW carriages, was rather unusual. *W. M. S. Jackson*

Far left: The Didcot to Winchester line was GW-owned but saw regular workings by Southern engines. It also brought Western locomotives into Southampton Terminus, notably *City of Truro* after her resurrection from York Museum. A strategic link between Southampton and the Midlands of great use in the two world wars, the line was little used by through traffic in peacetime which was mostly routed by way of Basingstoke and Reading. Class T9 No 30313 with a small six-wheeled tender drifts into Upton &

Blewby, the most northerly station on the branch, with the afternoon Southampton-Didcot train on 13 June 1959. *J. A. Coiley*

Left: 1930s Pullman elegance in the 1970s.

Above: An LSWR six-compartment suburban composite body No 0695 built by the Birmingham Railway Carriage & Wagon Co in 1885. Sold for use as a holiday chalet near Christchurch in 1921 after its 34ft long, six-wheel chassis was scrapped, it was brought to Corfe Castle station in May 1976 and later moved to Swanage where it is seen repainted in its original somewhat startling dark brown and salmon pink livery.

Below: An ex-SECR birdcage n/c brake/third and a Maunsell Thanet stock corridor brake third in departmental service, Clapham Junction.

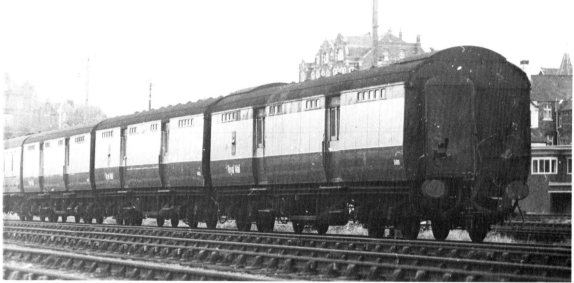

Top: S1562 — one of the last batch of four-wheel passenger luggage vans, built 1950, to what was essentially an SECR design No 1562 was fitted with a plywood body, and was at one time used as a security van. It is seen here at Micheldever after withdrawal in March 1979.

Above: Three Maunsell Post Office vans used on the Waterloo-Dorchester (later Weymouth) mail trains for over 30 years. The one nearest the camera is sorting van No 4919 built in 1936. Next to it is another sorting van No 4922 built 1939 and a stowage van of the 4947-60 series also built in 1939. The picture was taken at Weymouth in 1974 shortly before No 4919 was withdrawn and the others transferred to the Eastern Section. These, in turn were withdrawn in 1977 but at least one of the six Maunsell Post Office vans has been preserved. They were virtually the only Southern Railway designed carriages to receive blue and grey livery (other than emu stock).

Above: Former SR third No 1098, Sheffield Park, 30 January 1972. A 60ft, 32ton, 100-seat, 10-compartment carriage built by the SECR and intended for conversion to emu working. This never happened, instead it was converted to push-pull working in 1943, withdrawn in 1962 and bought by the Bluebell in 1963.

Below: Instruction car DS70155, converted in 1962 from 1930-built Maunsell corridor composite No 5600. At Norwood Junction, May 1972.

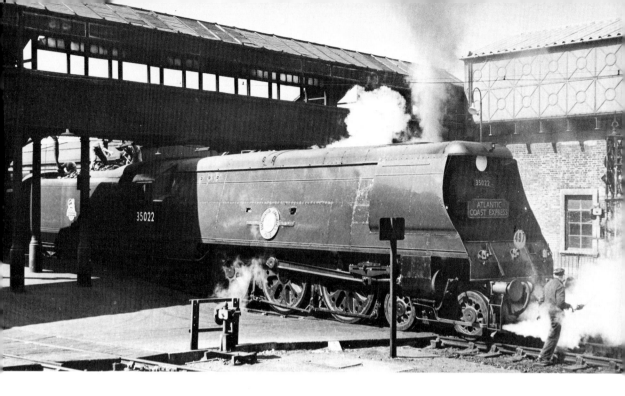

Top: The 'Atlantic Coast Express', that remarkable train with almost as many destinations as carriages, stands at Salisbury in June 1956 in the charge of 'Merchant Navy' No 35022 *Holland America Line*. G. F. Heiron

Above: Rebuilding of the 'Merchant Navys' began in 1956. Five years later *Holland America Line* in its destreamlined form was again in charge of the up 'Atlantic Coast Express', this time photographed at Worting, the junction of the Bournemouth and West of England lines $2\frac{1}{2}$ miles west of Basingstoke. The train carried through coaches from Ilfracombe, Torrington, Bude, Padstow, Plymouth, Sidmouth, Exmouth and Exeter. All but Plymouth, Exmouth and Exeter had lost their rail services by the 1970s and the last run of the 'Atlantic Coast Express' was at the end of the 1964 summer timetable.

Above: Rebuilt 'Merchant Navy' No 35008 *Orient Line* speeds past Worting junction with the 13.30 Waterloo-Bournemouth on 22 May 1961.

Below: Urie 'H15' mixed traffic 4-6-0 No 30487 passes under the Battledown viaduct at Worting junction on 8 September 1952 with a Plymouth to Nine Elms goods. I sometimes think Robert Urie has not received the acclaim he deserves. All his locomotives survived into the 1950s, and, most remarkably, his three classes of 4-6-0 for the LSWR, goods, mixed traffic, and express passenger, were all multiplied by his successor, and examples of the 'S15' and 'N15' classes have been preserved. *Brian Morrison*

Top: One of the most unusual and one of the most handsome types of locomotive employed on the Waterloo-Basingstoke semi-fasts was the 'N15X'. The seven locomotives of this class started out as 4-6-4Ts on the Brighton, the most successful of that impressive-looking but disappointing breed of mammoth Baltic tanks which enjoyed a brief vogue in the late 1910s and early 1920s. Electrification in the 1930s left them under-employed and so Eastleigh converted them to 4-6-0s and they spent the rest of their lives on the Western Section. Not as good as the 'Arthurs' or 'Nelsons' but better than the Drummond 'Paddleboxes', they settled down to secondary duties between Waterloo and Bournemouth and ended their days at Basingstoke in 1955/6. No 32328, *Hackworth*, gets a grip of his eight Bulleid corridors in the cutting east of Basingstoke on 15 September 1951. *P. M. Alexander*

Above: With the withdrawal of the Urie 'King Arthurs' their names, although not their nameplates, were transferred to 20 BR Standard Class 5 4-6-0s. No 73110 *The Red Knight*, stands at Basingstoke on 22 May 1961 with a train from the Eastern Region, waiting to follow out No 35012 *United States Line* on the 17.30 Waterloo-Bournemouth West. Basingstoke was at that time just beginning its expansion as a London overspill town. This, and its importance as the junction for Reading and the Midlands and the North of England, has enhanced its status as one of the busiest stations on the Southern Region.

Above: An unusual visitor to the Reading-Basingstoke service, and standing at the same platform where I had seen a GWR '61xx' 2-6-2T draw in with a rake of Hawksworth non-corridors on that sunny May evening 17 years earlier, was an Oxted line 3D Class 207 demu on an equally sunny July evening in 1978. Hampshire units normally work the hourly service on this line calling at Reading West, Mortimer, and Bramley, some extended beyond Basingstoke to Salisbury, although WR dmus also appear and as late as January 1980 I travelled the line in the last of the Reading-Tonbridge Tadpole units. Originally owned by the GWR, it is now Southern Region property as far as Wolvercote, the junction with the WR West of England main line, but it has always had a very joint flavour.

Below: Carriage destination boards survived on the Channel Islands boat trains and some of the inter-Regional expresses after they had vanished everywhere else. Hence the combination of such a board and blue and grey livery at Reading on a hot July day in 1972.

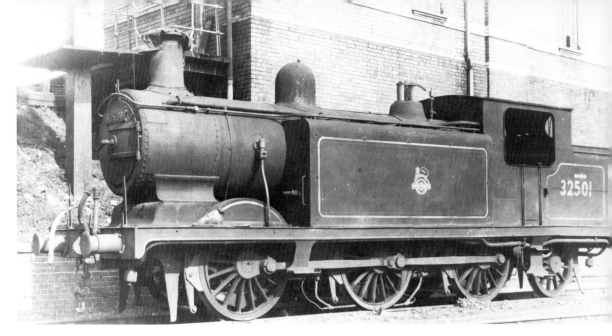

Above: Although Southern trains off the Basingstoke line have always used Reading General, those from Waterloo and Guildford had their own station, which was below and beside the Western one. In the 1950s the SR shed at Reading housed a rare collection of veterans from the LSW, the SEC and the LBSC railways. 'E4' No 32501, a representative of the most numerous class of the many LBSC 0-6-2Ts, is in store in March 1955. Behind is the now demolished GW Reading East main box. No 32501 was withdrawn in July of that year.

Below: Nowadays Southern Region trains use two platforms specially built for their use when the SR Reading station was closed (originally they had to make do with one, or cut across the WR main line). On 5 November 1979 4-CIG Class 421/2 forming the 22.32 to Waterloo stands as near as the Southern Region ever gets to HST travel, the 20.36 Weston super Mare to Paddington in the background being about to depart. The Victorian Italianate clocktower contrasts with the 1960s functional platform awnings.

Above right: In steam days Southern locomotives working over the Western Region carried the standard British headcodes, hence the two discs over the buffers on Urie 'N15' No 30736, *Excalibur*,

speeding through Tilehurst in the Thames Valley with the Bournemouth-Birkenhead train. This took the west curve at Reading, thus avoiding Reading General station, and engines were changed at Oxford.

Centre right: A rake of 11 Maunsell corridors in the charge of Churchward Mogul No 6313 of Didcot shed, forming a summer Saturday Portsmouth-Birmingham Snow Hill train, is held at the signals outside Banbury station on 8 August 1959. Such was the intensity of traffic that day that it was possible for the driver and passengers of this train to look forward and see the train ahead of them, and backward and see another train approaching the signals to the rear. The delays were something fearful.

Below right: Most trains between the Southern and Western Regions change locomotives at Reading although, as we have seen, Western Region locomotives regularly work south and Southern Region ones just as often work north, usually to Oxford. A '33' has just coupled up to a train from the Midlands at Reading whilst a 'Western' and an '08' stand on the through road in September 1969.

Above: In the early days of nationalisation Guildford like Reading was the last home of many old Victorian & Edwardian locomotives. In September 1951 No 30400, the last survivor of Drummond's 'S11' class, one of 10 6ft 4-4-0s designed for service in the West Country, stands under the coaling plant ahead of an Adams 'G6' 0-6-0T of 1894-1900 vintage, whilst on the adjacent line is one of the even longer-lived '0395' 0-6-0s of 1881-5 which retains its original rectangular cab windows. *Brian Morrison*

Below: Western Region 'Manor' 4-6-0s and Moguls regularly worked from the Southern station at Reading to Redhill although the carriages were always of Southern origin (except for inter-Regional trains). No 6312 arrives at Guildford towing an SECR birdcage set with a train from Redhill in April 1954. *Stanley Creer*

Left: Although passenger services on the Waterloo-Portsmouth line were electrified in 1937, goods services remained in the charge of steam, as on other Southern electrified main lines, until the 1960s. The SR never went in for goods locomotives to any great extent, its largest ones being the 'S15' class, 45 4-6-0s with 5ft 7in driving wheels; even so they were often found on passenger trains. The last of the class, No 30847, and the very last Maunsell 4-6-0, built in December 1936, wheels a Nine Elms-Fratton freight through Guildford on 6 April 1961. At that time No 30847 was shedded at Redhill. Withdrawn from Feltham in January 1964, she is now on the Bluebell Railway.

Below: Guildford on 20 August 1979: 4-VEP unit No 7715 leaving with the 18.30 Guildford-Waterloo as 'Tadpole' diesel-electric unit No 1203 arrives on a Reading-Tonbridge service. *Les Bertram*

Below: 'Lord Nelson' No 30854, *Howard of Effingham*, passes Durnsford Road on 23 August 1958 with down empty stock for Southampton Terminus. In the distance is Earlsfield station and on the left is Durnsford Road power station. The latter was built by the LSWR for the opening of its suburban electrification system in 1915. It had closed earlier in 1958 although it was some years before it was demolished.

Bottom: One of the Urie LSW 'S15s' of 1920-1 leaves Wimbledon in August 1958 with a summer Saturday train, No 30510 heads the 09.27 Wimbledon to Weymouth. The majority of the carriages are 'Ironclads', the final type of LSW corridor design and the forerunner of Maunsell designs for the Southern. *Stanley Creer*

Right: Rebuilt 'West Country' No 34046, *Braunton*, passes Wimbledon with the 15.20 Waterloo-Weymouth, 16 April 1960. The first five carriages are a set of the final type of Bulleids, built after nationalisation; the next two are Maunsells, one a restaurant car; and a three-coach BR standard set brings up the rear. Although a great many of the four-wheel PMVs (now classified NQV) of the type next to the engine are still in service they are hardly likely to be found on Inter-City expresses.

Below right: In 1971 the SR introduced the PEP (Class 445) experimental suburban units. From these were developed the whole range of modern suburban emus employed on the ER Great Northern section, on the LMR on Merseyside, around Glasgow and on the Southern (the 508s). Unit No 4001 stands in the sidings at Wimbledon in January 1979 shortly before transfer to departmental service.

Bottom right: 'M7' No 30248 on empty stock passes one of the augmented Maunsell 4-SUB units north of Earlsfield station, 6 June 1961. For many years the Drummond 'M7s', the most powerful 0-4-4Ts in Britain, were the mainstay of empty stock workings in and out of Waterloo. The first three carriages are a set of the earliest Bulleid corridors of 1945/6, of traditional side-corridor layout with separate doors to each compartment. Their close resemblance to the Bulleid suburban trailers in the train on the opposite track is clear. The motorcoaches of the emu are part of the first batch built by Maunsell for the Western Section in 1925, and based on the LSW units of 1915, although without their elaborate panelling. One has been preserved at the National Railway Museum at York.

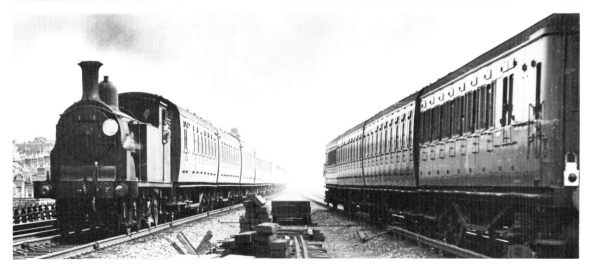

Top: Electrification of the Waterloo–Reading line in 1938 left steam still in charge of parcels duties, and consequently Reading veterans, many of non-LSW origin, continued to work into Waterloo. On 29 February 1952 No 31746, one of Wainwright's 'D' class 4-4-0s of 1901, generally considered the epitome of Edwardian elegance, stands ready to depart with the 20.13 to Reading. *Brian Morrison*

Above: A remarkable sight on 19 March 1961 was this ancient Adams 4-4-2T, representative of a class which began its days in the early 1880s on suburban services out of Waterloo and by 1920 had gone apart from three examples employed on the Lyme Regis branch and the East Kent Railway. No 30582 returned to her old haunts for an enthusiasts' special prior to withdrawal and stands alongside one of her successors three times removed. One of the three Adams 4-4-2Ts, LSWR No 488, survives on the Bluebell Railway. *Stanley Creer*

Above: No 30520, one of Urie's big 'H16' Pacific freight tanks of 1921-2 and sometimes used on empty stock workings, pulls out of Waterloo past Urie 'King Arthur' No 30751, *Etarre,* on a Bournemouth express, and 4-COR No 3145 leading a 12-coach Portsmouth train on 23 August 1952.   *Brian Morrison*

Below: New style Southern, 1980.

Above: 8 July 1961, No 30851, *Sir Francis Drake*, creates a fine smoke screen as he accelerates an 11-coach Bournemouth train through Vauxhall, made up of Bulleid six- and three-car sets with a couple of Maunsells at the front for the extra Saturday traffic.

Below: A rare refugee from the Eastern Section, displaced by electrification was ex-SECR 'C' class 0-6-0 No 31510, on empty stock on 1 July 1961. Indeed this was the only occasion I saw one on such duties. Big Ben and the Victoria Tower can be seen in the left background.

Top: With the Kent Coast electrification a number of 'Schools' returned to the Western Section for a few months before withdrawal. On 8 July 1961 No 30910, *Merchant Taylors*, in the charge of a Lymington Pier express — a duty which would have been the responsibility of a Drummond 4-4-0 some 10 years earlier — passes No 30918, *Hurstpierpoint*, backing down from Nine Elms to take out a Bournemouth train.

Above: Vauxhall on 16 February 1976 with a Hounslow train of two 2-EPBs (Class 416/2) pulling out and a 4-SUB (Class 405/2) on the right.

Above: One of the most familiar components of the Clapham Junction scene for over 30 years were the Portsmouth line express units of 1937. Variously known as the 'Nelsons' both on account of the Portsmouth link and their one-eyed look, and 'Belly Wobblers' on account of the movement of their corridor connections fore and aft, a typical 12-coach formation rattles south-westwards a few months before the 4-CIGs/4-BIGs (Class 421/420) took over in 1970.

Below: Waterloo was the last London terminus to succumb to regular main line diesels, 'Warships' taking over on the Exeter line in 1964.

Top: Not only did Clapham Junction offer the unending panorama of trains passing through the station, but there was the additional entertainment of shunting in the carriage sidings. Empty stock was constantly arriving from and departing for Waterloo and being remarshalled. This was chiefly the responsibility of the 'M7s' plus some half-dozen Brighton 'E4s', but a great many other types put in appearances — big tanks such as Urie 'H16s' and Maunsell 'Ws', and almost every type of tender engine which worked into Waterloo took a trip down to Clapham Junction. At the time I took this picture, November 1961, of No 30788, *Sir Urre of the Mount*, the recent completion of the electrification of the Kent Coast lines had released many Bulleid Pacifics for service on the Western Section. Consequently the days of the 'King Arthurs' were numbered, but although *Sir Urre of the Mount* was to be withdrawn three months later she looks well cared for, standing alongside the Pullmans of the 'Bournemouth Belle'.

Above: Clapham Junction, the busiest station in the world. Not one of the most distinguished pieces of railway architecture, but a great

place for watching the trains go by. Some 25 years before I took this picture in March 1979 I was train spotting at the far end of this platform and came as near as I hope I ever shall to witnessing a serious accident. The platform serves the up fast and relief South Western main lines. Just as a Guildford bound 4-SUB non-stop to Surbiton approached on the opposite line a porter on the adjacent platform lost control of a barrow, identical to the one in the picture, loaded with milk churns. It toppled over the edge and fell on the track. I saw the driver of the emu stand up in his cab in horror a second or so before his train hit the barrow. There was a bang and a cloud of brown smoke, the train rocked but miraculously held the rails and came to a halt just out of the station. Of the barrow and churns there was no sign although one of my friends claimed that a lady emerging from a phone box on the platform at the moment of impact was drenched in milk. There have been instances of fearful carnage caused in just such circumstances. Probably the speed and the heavy motor bogie prevented the train derailing. As it was, within three-quarters of an hour the track was clear and everything was back to normal.

Above: The two most easterly tracks on the Brighton side of Clapham Junction were not electrified as they were used by inter-Regional trains from the Kensington Olympia line. Class W 2-6-4T No 31920 pulls up the gradient with a transfer freight from Willesden to Norwood Yard. The 15 locomotives of this class were a familiar sight in the Clapham and Croydon areas, being shedded for almost all of their careers at Stewarts Lane, Hither Green and Norwood Junction. My earliest memories of them are in charge of coal trains for the Waddon Gas Works emerging from the gloomy depths of West Croydon station and trundling past the railings through which I would press my nose if permitted to stop by mother during shopping expeditions. *Brian Stephenson*

Below: A Johnson 0-6-0 of the London Midland Region, No 43261 of Cricklewood Shed trundles through Clapham Junction with a transfer goods off the West London line and heads for Feltham on 25 June 1951. *Brian Morrison*

Above: To the west of the Clapham Junction-Kensington Olympia line is another inter-Regional link, the Old Kew junction-Bollo Lane junction spur connecting the North & South Western Junction line with the Southern. One of Bulleid's strange-looking 'Q1' 0-6-0s, No 33010 of Feltham Shed, built at Brighton in 1942, crosses the Midland main line at Kentish Town on a bitterly cold, grey January day in 1960, heading back home from the Eastern Region. All the wagons visible are wooden-bodied, three of them carrying old style containers. No 33010 was withdrawn in January 1964.

Below: Away on the far side of the Western Section of Clapham Junction, the first of the Hastings line diesel-electric units runs through on 6 February 1957 on its way from Eastleigh to Ashford prior to entering service. Its slab-sided profile is very noticeable, a shape decreed by several narrow tunnels encountered between Tunbridge Wells and Bexhill. In the sidings on the right is a set of LSW non-corridors used to work the rush hour service to Kensington Olympia, chiefly for the benefit of Post Office workers. It was the last steam-hauled suburban service on the Southern. 'H' class 0-4-4Ts lasting on it until 1962, Standard 2-6-2Ts and 2-6-4Ts taking over until 1967. Today a '33'-hauled 4-TC set is most commonly employed. *R. C. Riley*

Below: The 'Brighton Belle' gets its water tanks refilled at Victoria's Platform 16. It should be added that the metal plates hanging over the doorways were removed before the train set off for Brighton. This 1970 picture shows the Pullmans in their final blue and grey livery.

Bottom: Standing at Victoria Station platform 10 on the Brighton side on 22 May 1959 is No 4501, an unusual 4-SUB set made up of two former LBSC and, nearest the camera, two ex-LSW carriages. Between 1925 and 1937 the Southern Railway brought out 321 three-car emus converted from LBSCR, SECR and LSWR stock, all of which except for some of the LBSC ones were originally steam-hauled. After the war they were either withdrawn or converted to four-car sets. Withdrawal continued as new Bulleid sets appeared and by the mid-1950s all had gone except for some particularly vintage-looking arc-roof ex-LBSC ones, the exception being the half-LSW No 4501.

Above: Much less well known than Clapham Junction but more accurately named is Clapham station, which really is in Clapham, Clapham Junction being in the heart of Wandsworth. Unit No 1803 is one of the oldest of all the Southern electric units, a two-car set converted from the original Brighton overhead electric stock of 1909 (the flattened roof over the guard's and driver's compartments is where the collectors were once fitted). It is seen on the Victoria-London Bridge service on 11 October 1953, where it worked for 46 years. The tracks to the right are those of the Eastern Section main line out of Victoria, whilst in the mist beyond the signals is Stewarts Lane Depot, Battersea Dogs Home and the South Western main line. *R. C. Riley*

Below: Three miles east of Clapham, past the now-vanished emu works where I caught my first sight of part of one of the prototype BR standard express emus (the CEPBs, as they were originally labelled in 1956), the South London line joins the Tulse Hill-London Bridge line at Peckham Rye. Clapham was once a rather superior residential district but it is hard to imagine that Peckham Rye and its station were ever anything even the most optimistic estate agent could have called desirable. Both have a certain ghastly Dickensian fascination and are probably marginally more salubrious today than in October 1953 when this picture was taken of a pointed-nosed LSW-built 4-SUB, No 4207, leading an eight-coach London Bridge-Crystal Palace Low Level-London Bridge train past the long vanished ex-LNW/Midland coal yard, full of wooden-bodied wagons. *R. C. Riley*

Above: London Bridge, midsummer 1952. Brighton Atlantic No 32426, *St Alban's Head*, pulls out with a rush-hour train for the Oxted line. Earle Marsh came to the Brighton from Doncaster in 1905 and in that year brought out his slightly modified version of Ivatt's large Atlantic, the 'H1' class. Six years later came the more powerful 'H2s', externally modified by a straight running plate from cylinders to rear driving wheels, a feature which perfected an already very handsome design. I remember both the 'H1s' and the 'H2s' in the postwar malachite green livery and thought they looked quite splendid. All the 'H1s' and one of the 'H2s' had gone by mid-1951 but the five survivors were repainted in lined black, a less spectacular livery but nevertheless one that suited them well.

Shedded at Brighton and always well cared for, they worked up to London Bridge and Victoria via the Oxted line, up the main line to Kensington and Willesden Junction on summer Saturdays, on the coast line with the Bournemouth and Exeter expresses, and still put in the odd appearance on their old favourite, the Newhaven Boat Train. *Brian Morrison*

Below: Tower blocks loom over a much modernised London Bridge on a wet November evening in 1979 at the beginning of the rush-hour. In the foreground leading a 12-coach Eastbourne and Hastings train is 4-CIG (Class 421/1) No 7324, one of the units built in 1965 to replace the Southern Railway express units of 1933/5.

Top: First station out of London Bridge on the Brighton line is New Cross Gate. Southern trains connect here with London Transport's East London line, a useful link with dockland and the East End. There was a physical connection between LT and SR tracks in early BR days, although regular through trains had long ceased, but this has now been removed. An LT train from Whitechapel arrives in March 1979 passing a 4-EPB (Class 415/1) and a 4-CEP (Class 411) in the sidings.

Above: 4-SUB (Class 405/2) No 4295 on a Dorking-London Bridge working pulls into Sydenham in February 1979. The line on the left disappearing into the snowstorm leads to Crystal Palace. The platforms, which as at other inner suburban stations between Norwood Junction and New Cross Gate, serve only the slow lines, are staggered. It was near here that Claude Monet painted the railway scene in the 1870s, some of his many thrilling pictures of London.

Above: Tulse Hill, three miles west of Sydenham. 'E1' 4-4-0 No 31067 standing beside an impressive bank of signals enlivens the usually mundane all-electric Sunday morning scene on 22 May 1960 with a special from London Bridge to Eastleigh via the Didcot, Newbury and Winchester line.

Left: No 32424, *Beachy Head*, the last Atlantic in service on British Railways, runs past suburban back gardens at Norbury on its final run on 13 April 1958, the train being an RCTS special of boat train stock from Victoria to Newhaven. Brighton Atlantics had been associated with the Newhaven Boat Trains for the best part of 50 years and on that day *Beachy Head* performed with all her old flair and competence. It is churlish to regret missed preservation opportunities when one considers what remarkable things have been achieved, but still it would have been nice if the efforts to save *Beachy Head* had succeeded.

Right: Thornton Heath, for many years my local station, is typical of those built in the early years of the present century when the tracks were quadrupled between Selhurst and Balham. A substantial four-platform affair built of London stock brick and with plenty of the original decorative engraved glass, which somehow survived the blitz of 1940 and the flying bombs of 1944 when more damage was inflicted on what was then the County Borough of Croydon than on any other part of London or the south-east. There were up and down goods yards where Billinton radials used to shunt — my father remembers their Stroudley predecessors in their original yellow livery — both now closed; the buildings on the up fast platform have been demolished and colour-lights have replaced the semaphores, the arms of which would often clump down within a few inches of one's nose as one crossed the footbridge after alighting from a down train.

Right: An Epsom Downs-Victoria train approaches Thornton Heath. Just round the bend is Selhurst. Both stations, together with Norwood Junction, do great business when Crystal Palace are playing at home, the ground being visible from the two former stations. Now in the First Division, Crystal Palace when I first become a supporter used regularly to have to apply for re-admission to the Fourth Division. Nevertheless the team has always attracted considerable support and not even the trams with their enormous capacity, which rattled over the bridge under which the 4-SUB is about to pass, could cope with the crowds and many people would walk the mile or so from the ground to the station.

Above: Two of the original Bulleid 4-SUB units of 1945 in the sidings at Crystal Palace in September 1970. The domed roofs over the cabs gave them an appearance almost identical to the 2-HALs, and like them they paid scant attention to passenger comfort. Each four-car unit has a seating capacity of no less than 460. Perhaps Bulleid hoped to hasten the advent of the permissive society for in a crowded train the upright seats and minimal amount of leg room brought a passenger into intimate contact both with those sitting opposite and on either side. They were on a par with the notorious 'sit up and beg' Gresley suburban sets. Since then things have gradually improved, the latest Great Northern electrics and the Southern 508s being the greatest advance of all. Crystal Palace used to have two stations; the one illustrated, despite being at a considerable elevation, was the Low Level one. Crystal Palace High Level was the terminus of an SEC branch from Nunhead. The decline and finally destruction by fire of the Crystal Palace reduced the branch's usefulness and it closed in 1954. Nevertheless, there was considerable opposition to its disappearance and it is now generally considered to have been a mistake for there was always a certain amount of commuter traffic. The station itself was a very grand establishment, with an overall roof echoing the Palace itself. It remained, for some years after closure, a derelict, haunted place, silent except for the echoing bang of a broken door or window swinging in the wind which gusted through the shattered roof, and so richly evocative of its long-past Victorian heyday that had the ghosts of the crowds which once flocked through it on their way to the wonders within and without the great glass palace opposite suddenly materialised one would hardly have been surprised.

Above: For 30 years almost all the express workings on the Central Section between London and Hastings, Eastbourne, Brighton and Littlehampton were the prerogative of the 6-PUL and 6-PAN units. The heavy metal-bodied motorcoaches were handsome looking vehicles and had lots of nice dignified wooden panelling and deep cushioned seats, but, oh dear, their riding could be diabolical. The trailers, except for the Pullmans, were very similar to contemporary steam stock and had canvas covered roofs (an anachronistic but seemingly quite serviceable feature perpetuated on new Bulleid main line carriages into BR days). 6-PUL No 3006 leads a Brighton non-stop on 9 March 1965 through the unfamiliar surroundings of West Norwood, having been diverted from the main line by a goods train derailment at Streatham Common. *Brian Stephenson*

Below: The only blue and yellow liveried example of its type was this 6-COR No 3045, seen at Selhurst in October 1968. The motorcoach is from a 6-PAN unit and the different window design can be compared with the 6-PUL unit . Twelve of these 6-CORs were formed in 1966/7 from withdrawn PUL/PAN sets and sent to work on the Kent Coast commuter services, an unlikely part of the system on which to end their days. They then rarely appeared on the Central Section although I did see two passing through Norwood Junction in September 1968 and they came into Selhurst Depot for attention from time to time. All were taken out of service by the end of 1968; one of the trailer coaches survives on the Nene Valley Railway.

Top: There is a remarkable series of junctions in the triangle between Selhurst, East Croydon and Norwood Junction. Equally remarkable was the upwards growth of Croydon in the 1960s when tower blocks seemed to spring up almost overnight. 4-EPB (Class 415/1) No 5188 negotiates the Selhurst maze on a West Croydon-Crystal Palace-Victoria working in March 1974, dwarfed by the Manhattan-like background. The 4-EPBs were introduced in late 1951. Their body design, apart from the cab, was virtually identical to this later 4-SUBs but the electropneumatic brakes, control gear, and buckeye couplers were a considerable advance. Nevertheless, liked many of the Bulleid 4-SUBs they were built on underframes from withdrawn wooden-bodied units, and in March

1979 I noted one at Clapham Junction with LSW stamped on both axleboxes of the leading bogie of one of the motorcoaches.

Above: A remarkable survivor into the 1970s was this Mobile Classroom seen at Selhurst Depot in 1970. Once 3-SUB No 1782, formed in 1930 from ex-LSW suburban steam stock, it went into departmental service in 1956 and in due course acquired blue livery with yellow ends. It was withdrawn in 1974 and one really does feel that the historic importance of the unit ought to have been officially appreciated and that it should have become part of the National Collection.

Above: 2-BIL No 2057 on a Victoria stopping train at East Croydon in the spring of 1971, the year the last of the BILs was withdrawn. This was a rare suburban working for the type although they were occasionally pressed into emergency suburban service at the end of their careers.

Below: The 4-CORs, although originally employed on the ex-LSW route to Portsmouth and the Mid-Sussex line of the former LBSC, were soon used to a limited extent on the Brighton, Worthing and Littlehampton lines. A 12-coach train with No 3110 leading, in blue livery but not yet with all-yellow ends, hurries down the main line through South Croydon on a rush-hour London Bridge-Littlehampton express in May 1967.

Top: The East Croydon pilot, 'O1' No 31048, at the north end of the station, 13 May 1959. A Wainwright rebuild of a Stirling South Eastern design of 1878, the class was extraordinarily long-lived. No 31048 was one of the last three survivors, one of which has been preserved.

Above: An East Grinstead-Victoria train approaches East Croydon in a January snowstorm in 1971. There is a close resemblance between the 3H (Class 205) demus and the 2-EPB emus just as there was between Maunsell steam and electric stock of the 1930s. Dieselisation came to the Oxted line in 1962 when the first of the 19 units especially built for this service appeared. They are variously known as Class 207, 3D, and East Sussex units, the last being distinctly inaccurate as they spend most of their time in Surrey. There were nothing like enough of them to replace all the steam workings on the Oxted line and they were supplemented by a number of the older Hampshire units plus four locomotive-hauled trains which appear during the rush-hour.

Right: 2-EPB (Class 416/2) No 5773 at West Croydon in 1970 about to set off over the single track line to Wimbledon. The 2-EPBs of 1954-6 were the first BR Standard units built for the Southern, being principally intended to strengthen Eastern Section rush-hour trains to 10 coaches, but they also replaced the old ex-Overhead two-car units on the South London and West Croydon-Wimbledon lines.

Above: At South Croydon the Oxted line diverges and climbs steeply into the North Downs whilst the Brighton line continues down the valley past Purley before tunnelling through the Downs beyond Coulsdon. From their introduction in 1951 until the end of steam the Brighton-built Standard 2-6-4Ts dominated Oxted services. No 80152, then scarcely one year old and shedded since new at Brighton, pulls up the bank from South Croydon towards Selsdon station on 1 April 1958 with the 13.08 Victoria to Tunbridge Wells West.

Below: Twenty-one years later a 3H demu leads a Victoria-East Grinstead train up the bank. Although the platforms remain the buildings on the Oxted line side of Selsdon station have been demolished, but a gas lamp survives to provide a minimal amount of light for passengers for the Elmers End-Sanderstead rush-hour-only emu service.

Left: All three Southern Railway constituents were great believers in the 0-4-4T for suburban work. Electrification ended their days on such duties and in later years they came to epitomise rural branch line motive power in Kent, Sussex, Surrey, Hampshire, the Isle of Wight and the West Country. Wainwright's SEC 'H' class of 1904-5 were pretty little engines with their distinctive cabs with overhanging eaves and they were long used on the Oxted line. The line was built jointly by the LBSC and the SEC the influence of both companies was still much in evidence in the 1950s. No 31520 with a neat collection of briquettes in her bunker makes a perfect South Eastern picture with her birdcage set as she approaches Riddlesdown Tunnel on 10 June 1954 with an up East Grinstead train.   *E. R. Wethersett*

Above: A photograph taken at the same spot seven years later, 19 June 1961. An unusually dirty Standard tank, No 80094, heads the 17.38 Victoria to East Grinstead. The birdcage sets had gone by now, but a few loose SEC design carriages still appeared to strengthen rush-hour trains. All were withdrawn by the end of 1962.

Above left: A little earlier on that warm June evening in 1961, 'D1' 4-4-0 No 31739 came by on the 16.48 Victoria to Brighton via Eridge, Uckfield and Lewes. SEC 4-4-0s had long been associated with the Oxted line but this was possibly the very last appearance by one. The Kent Coast electrification was complete and the few surviving inside-cylinder 4-4-0s performed little work in the few weeks left to them. I had seen No 31739 on the same train the day before but the next day a 'Schools' was in charge and remained so for some weeks. The train consists of a Hastings four-car set and one of the very handsome three-car sets built in 1936 for Kent Coast services.

Left: 'Schools' No 30901, *Winchester*, was a regular performer at this time on the 16.40 London Bridge to Brighton, although the class had only rarely been seen on the line before the first stage of the Kent Coast electrification. The full first from the BR Standard set was undergoing repair, hence the elderly Maunsell replacement.

Below left: A '33' emerges from Oxted Tunnel (one of the many on the line) with a rush-hour East Grinstead-London Bridge train in June 1977. Oxted was a village below the Pilgrims Way until the railway arrived in the 1880s. Old Oxted remains much as it was but a small town grew up around the station. Station Road West has some gems of architecture in the Mock Tudor style including the cinema, would you believe, and from the turn of the century many large villas were built amongst the trees above the tunnel and elsewhere. For 50 years electrification has been promised and the building of large numbers of private and some council houses in the 1960s increased the demand for this. With the closure of the lines south of Uckfield and East Grinstead the route has become virtually an outer suburban one but it still waits for the third-rail.

Above: Hurst Green is the junction for the East Grinstead and Uckfield lines. On 13 May 1950 ex-LBSC 'I3' 4-4-2T No 32022 approaches the halt with a train from Haywards Heath via the Bluebell line and East Grinstead. The superheated 'I3s' were perhaps the most famous of all British express tanks. Put on the Sunny South Coast Express between Brighton and Willesden Junction in 1909, the 'I3s' amazed the profligate LNWR with the ease and economy with which they performed the task. As a consequence the Premier Line enthusiastically adopted superheating and by the Grouping it had become a feature of all large British locomotives. The LBSC went on to build Pacific and Baltic passenger tanks, all excellent machines but none which had quite the same impact as the 'I3s'. *E. R. Wethersett*

Below: By the time this picture was taken at the same spot in 1970, of a '3D' (Class 207) demu on an East Grinstead-Victoria working, the old lower-quadrant LBSC semaphore was the last of its type in use on the Southern Region. The house in the left background is one of a terrace of railway cottages, then being renovated and subsequently sold to private occupiers. Despite trains running past both back and front gardens they were snapped up, perhaps by railway enthusiasts, who knows? In the early 1960s, in recognition of the boom in house building in this desirable part of the Stockbroker belt, the old wooden Hurst Green Halt was replaced by a neat, much larger station with platforms capable of taking the nine-car diesel trains then entering service.

Above: Class H No 31278 pulls into Tunbridge Wells West with an auto-train from Oxted, 3 June 1961. In steam days through trains ran between Tunbridge Wells West and Victoria, and to London Bridge during the rush-hour, by way of the single track line through Forest Row to East Grinstead, whilst auto-trains took the alternative double-track route by way of Hever and Edenbridge, connecting with the through trains at Oxted. With dieselisation all London traffic was concentrated on Tunbridge Wells Central on the Charing Cross-Hastings line, and the West station is now served only by a Tonbridge-Eridge shuttle service which connects at either end with London trains.

Left: Track relaying on the Hurst Green to Edenbridge and Uckfield line. In 1969 closure notices were posted but, recognising the increasing commuter potential all along the route, permission was refused. Somewhat surprisingly the section between Uckfield and Lewes was closed, thus ending the line's potential as a diversionary route between London and the coast, although this was admittedly limited while it remained non-electric.

Above: 'I3' No 32091 swings round into East Grinstead High Level with a train from Victoria. The last built of the 'I3s', she entered service from Brighton shed in March 1913. The LMS type 2-6-4Ts introduced on the Central Section in 1950 brought the 'I3s' ' career to an abrupt end. No 32091 was the last to be withdrawn, being taken out of service from Brighton shed in May 1952. However she survived for the Works Centenary celebrations in the autumn and was not broken up until February 1953, the deed being done at Ashford.
E. R. Wethersett

Left: A '33' stands in the sidings at the south end of East Grinstead station in June 1970. Once a busy junction where four lines connected, by this date all but the London line had disappeared. Beyond the locomotive is the viaduct which once carried the tracks of the Haywards Heath and Lewes line. Now used to stable locomotive-hauled rush-hour stock, steam trains hauled by Brighton-built tank engines may once again cross it if the Bluebell Railway succeeds in its long battle for permission to extend north of Horsted Keynes.

Above: Sheffield Park in BR days with No 42101, one of the LMS type Fairburn 2-6-4Ts built at Brighton, but later exchanged with the Scottish Region for Standard 2-6-4Ts, at the head of a Brighton-East Grinstead train. *R. C. Riley*

Below: SECR reincarnation on the Bluebell. The little 'P' class 0-6-0Ts of 1909 led undistinguished lives on the SEC, SR and BR, but four out of the eight have nevertheless survived. Three are on the Bluebell, one of which is currently on loan to the East Somerset Railway, one on the Kent & East Sussex Railway. Bluebell's No 27, the spring sunshine glinting on her brass dome, her paintwork sparkling, bustles along with two ex-SEC carriages. The first is No 1050, a fascinating vehicle in that it is a Southern Railway conversion on a Lancing built underframe of 1927 of two (possibly three) South Eastern six-wheelers of the early 1880s. The rear vehicle is No 1061, one of the classic Wainwright birdcage brakes, built in 1909 and once part of a three-car set.

Below: This rather extraordinary notice was to be found beside the level crossing at Barcombe Mills, the last station on the Uckfield-Lewes line, and close to the junction with the line from Sheffield Park. A haunt of fishermen who came out from Lewes and Brighton to try their luck in the River Ouse, the railway runs down the Ouse valley all the way from Buxted, now the penultimate station on the Uckfield line and once a centre of the Sussex iron industry, to Lewes, and, indeed, right to the river mouth at Newhaven. Iron-working was once the principal industry of the Sussex Weald but it ceased just as the railway age was dawning, although it is worth noting that the first railway in the south-east was the Surrey Iron Railway, relics of which were uncovered close to the present Brighton line at Merstham during the construction of the M23 motorway.

Below: The last train of the day approaches Horsted Keynes, 25 July 1980. *David Eatwell*

Bottom: Sheffield Park in January 1974 looking towards Horsted Keynes, with a 'P' class standing at the up platform. The Bluebell inherited a station little changed since its building in 1882, a particularly fine tile-hung house typical of many found in the Sussex Weald. Bullhead rails, wood and iron pailings, and gas lamps all remained to help recreate the atmosphere of Victorian and Edwardian days which has been such a joy to film-makers over the years.

BRITISH RAILWAYS NOTICE

WHEN THE NEIGHBOURING ROADS ARE FLOODED PERSONS MAY PASS ON FOOT AT THEIR OWN RISK OVER THE BRITISH TRANSPORT COMMISSIONS STRIP OF LAND 6 FEET WIDE ON THE NORTH WEST SIDE OF THE HEDGE FROM THE GATE TO THE STILE TO THE FOOTPATH CROSSING THE PATHWAY. AT OTHER TIMES THE GATE WILL BE KEPT LOCKED BY THE PARISH COUNCIL.

THE BRITISH TRANSPORT COMMISSION RESERVE THE RIGHT TO TERMINATE THIS ARRANGEMENT WITHOUT NOTICE.

Above: 'D' class 4-4-0 No S1574 of Ashford shed approaches Hailsham with an Eastbourne-Tunbridge Wells West train on 6 September 1950. The first coach is ex-LSW, the rest ex-SEC. Known as the Cuckoo line following the tradition that the first cuckoo was heard in the vicinity each spring, this single-track route enabled those who cared about such things to travel by through steam train from Eastbourne to London for a further 20 years after the main line had been electrified, just as the Bluebell line allowed Brighton eccentrics a similar facility. It took a lot longer but the scenery was very nice. *E. R. Wethersett*

Below: 3H unit No 1120 pulls out of Hailsham for Eastbourne just before closure in 1968 and after the line north of Hailsham to Eridge had already gone. The Hailsham-Polegate-Eastbourne trains were always well patronised and were both quicker and cheaper than the bus. An enquiry into the closure was held at which it was stated that the population would have to reach a certain figure before the service would become viable. Despite the fact that hundreds of homes were under construction and plans for many more were approved which would — and within two years did — take the population well over the required figure, the tracks were ripped up.

Above: A Brighton-Hastings stopping train of two 2-BILs leaves Polegate for Eastbourne in September 1969. The BILs were handsome units, both inside and out, and if they didn't give as good a ride as modern BR stock they were better than most of their contemporaries. Between 1935 and 1938 152 2-BILs were built and they worked all over the electrified tracks of the Western and Central Sections, although the only time I ever saw any on the Eastern was in late 1969 when I came across a rake awaiting breaking-up at Charlton, close to where so many London trams and trolleybuses had met their end. The inverted triangle indicates the guard's van end of the unit.

Below: A Class 73 electro-diesel draws a rake of condemned 2-BILs into Polegate in June 1969. These were three of the first 10 units, delivered early in 1935 for the Eastbourne and Hastings semi-fast services, and distinguishable from the remainder by the louvres over the doors and the not quite flush fitting windows. The middle unit has acquired a later trailer. At one time Polegate was an important junction with a goods yard where shunting went on 24 hours a day. But the drift of goods traffic to the roads and the closure of the Hailsham and the direct Eastbourne avoiding lines meant that by 1970 it had ceased to be a junction at all. Eventually the station itself and the handsome signalbox were demolished, the station being rebuilt on a smaller scale nearer the village centre.

Above: A variety of carriages and liveries at Eastbourne in September 1970. From right to left 4-VEP (Class 423) No 7803 in its original blue livery with raised metal BR symbol; 4-BIG (Class 420/1) No 7047 newly repainted in blue and grey (the original CIGs and BIGs came out in green but were repainted in 1968-70 in blue and grey, none of them — unlike all the other contemporary BR standard emus — having ever been blue); a set of Eastern Region locomotive-hauled Mk I stock for a Senior Citizens' holiday special, some of the carriages in maroon; and a Brighton train made up of two 2-BILs. The rear set is in blue, the front, No 2100, in green. No 2100 had its war-damaged trailer replaced by a postwar HAL type.

Below: Although the Southern, like all other Regions, uses '08' shunters, it also possesses all 26 of the '09' class, an uprated version of the '08' unique to the Southern. In June 1979 No 09.017 shunts a trainload of new Ford Transits over the Brighton-Eastbourne road at Newhaven and under the bridge which was to replace the level crossing. Newhaven owes its prosperity as a port to the railway. The LBSC inaugurated its Dieppe service in 1849 and by the end of the 19th century had spent over £½million improving the port, the most spectacular of its works being the 1,000yd long western breakwater. The passenger service continues to do good business but it is unfortunate that none of the extensive container traffic goes by train.

Above: Ex-LBSC 'D3' class 0-4-4T No 32390 at Brighton, 21 June 1955, with a Horsham push-pull; the coaches are also ex-LBSC. No 32390 was the last survivor of a class of 36 locomotives, designed by Robert Billinton in the 1890s. Replaced by LMS type and Standard 2-6-4Ts, all had gone by 1956. There were seven varieties of 0-4-4T inherited by the Southern Region, the 'D3' being the only ex-Brighton one. The single-track Brighton-Horsham line left the coast line at Shoreham and meandered through the South Downs by way of Bramber and Steyning to a junction with the Mid-Sussex line at Christ's Hospital, the latter station named after the boys' public school which moved down to Sussex from London in the 1890s. All that survives of the branch is a short section serving the cement works at Beedings beside the River Adur.
E. R. Wethersett

Below: A very unlikely meeting. The old Pullman works at Preston Park north of Brighton station were for some years used to store preserved BR stock. All have now gone elsewhere, and one which is restored to working order is *Evening Star*. But in 1972 she was towed in to take part in one of the displays put on by BR from time to time at Brighton station. No 92220 is standing next to the Waterloo & City's departmental 0-4-0 No DS75, with 4-COR No 3102 arriving from Eastbourne. The Sussex Coastway services provided the 4-CORs with their last duties, which ceased at the end of September 1972. On 1 October of that year No 3102 was one of two units which made a farewell tour of the Eastern Section. One 4-COR, No 3142 is preserved, rather oddly, on the Nene Valley line, where it spends its time being propelled by various unlikely foreign steam locomotives, a far cry from its duties on the Southern. It is perhaps surprising that none of the 4-COR trailers were preserved elsewhere. Whilst designed for electric traction they would certainly not have looked out of place in the charge of a Southern steam engine.

Top left: Symbol of Southampton — a July 1947 view of Herbert Walker Avenue in the docks with the RMS *Queen Mary* and an 0-6-0T passing on a freight. *Frank E. Moss*

Left: As dated a shot as the one above — a memory of the 'Night Ferry' as sleeping cars go aboard the *St Germain* at Dover. *BR*

Top right: The full-size replica of Sir Francis Drake's *Golden Hind* and three Sealink ferries, *Maid of Kent*, *Earl Godwin* and *Caledonian Princess* at Weymouth, 12 October 1980.

Above: PS *Ryde* one of the last Sealink paddle steamers raised up out of the water awaiting disposal at Newhaven in the winter of 1970-1. The *Ryde* was a 566ton triple expansion steamer built by Denny Brothers of Dumbarton in 1937 for the Portsmouth-Ryde service.

Above: No 32421, *South Foreland*, undergoing repairs inside Brighton Works on 2 November 1954. On the right a BR Standard 2-6-4T takes shape. Brighton Works produced its first locomotive in 1852 and closed for locomotive purposes in March 1958. Its site is now a car park. Locomotive building ceased after the Grouping but under Bulleid was renewed and continued into BR days, the great majority of the Standard 2-6-4Ts being built there. *Brian Morrison*

Below: Ashford Works, 22 May 1954. No 32570 was one of four Robert Billinton 'E5' passenger 0-6-2Ts of 1902-4, rebuilt with C3 boilers in 1911. In Southern Railway and BR days many LBSC-built engines were repaired either at Ashford or Eastleigh. No 32570 was the last of her class, being withdrawn in January 1956. In the background a Maunsell Mogul is under repair whilst also in view is an 'H' class cab. *Brian Morrison*

Below: Brighton Atlantic No 32425 *Trevose Head* at Brighton on 6 August 1956 with the Bournemouth express. The day before she had worked the last Atlantic-hauled Newhaven boat train, in both directions, although Newhaven Shed, so long associated with the Atlantics, had closed the year before. The Bournemouth train was a fairly regular turn of the Atlantics. They spent periods in store but always came out in the summer and at Christmas for the parcels traffic. Bogie failure brought about their end and by the date of this picture *Trevose Head* and *Beachy Head* were the only two of the class still active. *Trevose Head* went a month later, leaving *Beachy Head* to survive until April 1958.

Bottom: Two 'C2X' 0-6-0s stand outside Three Bridges Shed, 13 October 1956. The 45 locomotives of this class were the maids of all work on secondary goods services on the Central Section. Built by Vulcan in 1893-1902 and reboilered by Marsh, they were both

as familiar and as unremarkable a part of the Brighton line scene as the third rail and the Clayton Windmills. They also seemed as permanent but after 60 years dieselisation caught up with them. The second dome on No 32438 used to house the topfeed and although Maunsell removed the apparatus the second dome remained as a distinctive feature on many Brighton engines. In the background, undergoing minor repairs, is 'K' class 2-6-0 No 32348, one of a class of 17 engines designed by L. B. Billinton to replace the 'C2Xs' on the heaviest main line goods duties. This they did and remained so employed until withdrawn in November and December 1962, and although they were often seen on passenger workings they were not true mixed traffic engines in the manner of the Maunsell Moguls. Three Bridges Depot was situated just south of the junction of the Mid-Sussex and Brighton lines, and until Crawley New Town crept up towards it in the late 1950s, was surrounded by fields. Despite electrification it retained a number of passenger turns, on the East Grinstead and Oxted lines in particular.

Left: Making a journey it had done more than 62,000 times before, the 'Brighton Belle' thunders up the main line on an August evening in 1967. In the distance are the South Downs and the portals of Clayton Tunnel.

Below: Two 4-LAVs pull into Hassocks on a Brighton-Victoria stopping train, August 1967. Of all the Southern Railway emus, the 4-LAVs stuck most faithfully to their appointed task. Introduced in 1932 some months before electrification had reached Brighton, the last 4-LAV was withdrawn early in 1969. In all that time sorties off the Brighton line semi-fast and slow services was rare. None ever acquired British Rail blue livery and only one was repainted with all-yellow ends. They were handsome vehicles, and comfortable within the limits imposed by the indifferent riding qualities common to all Southern Railway-built emus, and by the lack of corridor accommodation in three out of four coaches in each unit. Two lavatories were to be found in the corridor trailer composite but none elsewhere, despite the unit's designation. The Southern Railway had a bit of an obsession with the toilet provision on its main line semi-fast and slow emus and named them accordingly; apart from the 4-LAVs there were the 2-NOLs which meant no lavatories, the BILs — Bi or two — and the 2-HALs, which didn't mean half a lavatory (although judging by the general standard of accommodation in those particular units it could well have done) but rather half the unit with lavatory access.

Bottom: Eight years after the original batch had entered service a final two 4-LAVs appeared early in 1940. They perpetuated the layout of the 1932 sets but in appearance and general appointments they were identical to the contemporary 2-HALs. No 2954 leads one of the 1932 sets through Balcombe Forest on a sunny summer day in 1967.

Above: The Newhaven Boat Train speeds through Balcombe Forest, 8 November 1950. The carriages have been newly painted in red and cream, apart from the Pullman, and the locomotive is No 20003, a 1,470hp Co-Co electric designed by English Electric and Raworth of the Southern. This was a slightly modified version of Nos 20001/2 built during the war. All three regularly worked the boat train for some 20 years until their withdrawal in 1969, the rest of their duties being chiefly freight work on the Mid-Sussex and Brighton lines. *British Rail*

Left: The first of the 2-BILs No 2001 (originally 1891) rattles out of Balcombe Tunnel on 23 June 1956 at the head of a Victoria-Eastbourne extra. Although this unit and its nine brothers were intended for Eastbourne and Hastings line workings when introduced in 1935 almost all through services to and from London quickly became the preserve of the express 6-PUL/PANs, the BILs taking themselves off to the Horsted Keynes-Haywards Heath-Lewes-Seaford and Brighton-Lewes-Eastbourne-Hastings stoppers. This therefore must have been a summer special and the patrons could think themselves lucky they were not cooped up in a wooden bodied, hard-riding pre-Grouping 4-SUB which might easily have been their lot on such an occasion. *Stanley Creer*

Below: A Victoria-Brighton stopping train composed of two 4-LAVs, with No 2947 leading, leaves the old Gatwick Airport station on 18 May 1958. Gatwick was originally a very small aerodrome with a grass runway next door to the racecourse, which also had a station, a mile or so to the north. *R. C. Riley*

Above: There were plans in existence to extend the aerodrome but when Crawley New Town was set up immediately after the war it was announced that an international airport was 'quite incompatible with the proper development of the new town'. Which didn't stop the plans coming to fruition. The racecourse was taken over, new terminal buildings erected alongside the old racecourse station, the A23 London to Brighton road was diverted under the terminal building so that the runways could be lengthened, the racecourse station was extensively rebuilt and incorporated into the terminal building, and the original airport station closed. A special train service was inaugurated and the seven postwar 2-HALs, Nos 2693-9 (but not the eighth, No 2700) were allocated to it, being detached and attached from and to Mid-Sussex line trains. A terminal was also built over platforms 15/16 at Victoria and Gatwick trains were usually routed into platform 15 with the special 2-HAL units nearest the barrier. One of these units is seen straying from its normal duties at the head of a Seaford-Lewes train near Southease & Rodmell.

Top: Eventually 4-VEPs (Class 423) took over from the HALs. They first appeared on the Bournemouth line and the earlier units were rare visitors to the Central Section whilst still in their original all-blue livery. Nevertheless No 7710 put in an appearance at Gatwick in the spring of 1969.

Above: In 1978 12 VEPs were given extra luggage accommodation and reclassified 4-VEG (G for Gatwick) (Class 427). They were also adorned with a luminous strip above the windows which bore the legend 'Rapid City Link Gatwick London'. In the Autumn of 1979 much bolder markings were introduced and newly repainted No 7907 stands so bedecked beside the terminal building on 1 November 1979. As Gatwick Airport has grown bigger and busier the enormous advantage of its rail link has become ever more apparent. More and more trains call, there is a service all through the night and through trains to the North of England were introduced in 1979. Would that Heathrow was so fortunate.

Above left: No 30909, *St Pauls*, pulls out of Redhill with the 15.04 to Reading on 17 March 1961. Guildford Shed had recently acquired No 30909 along with two others of the class, although all were withdrawn by the end of the following year. The class had often been seen on the Redhill-Tonbridge line but had previously been uncommon on the Redhill-Reading section. Standing in the sidings is No 33034 attached to a cattle truck, the latter a quite vanished piece of rolling stock on the Southern. Like No 30909, the four-coach set of Maunsell corridors had been displaced from the Hastings line.

Centre left: Steam haulage survived on the Tonbridge-Reading line until 1964, just about the last in south-east England. The route was scheduled for closure under Beeching but was reprieved and allocated six unique and curious 'Tadpole' demus. No 1203 is seen passing the site of Crowhurst junction on the 18.49 Tonbridge-Reading in June 1973. There had been a spur from here down to the Oxted-East Grinstead line which passes under the Tonbridge-Redhill line just beyond the milepost in the middle distance.

Bottom left: One of the infuriating features of the 'Tadpoles' was that the ex-emu driving trailer was almost always locked as, lacking any corridor connection, tickets couldn't be checked by the conductor/guard. This didn't matter too much in off-peak times, but during rush-hours, particularly on the Reading-Guildford section, overcrowding was chronic. There were therefore few regrets when Western Region dmus began to take over in 1979. One stands at

Redhill in June 1979. Those who complain about dmus can have little experience of Southern demus with their tendency to vibrate, generally rougher ride and absence of forward vision. The view opened up from the front and rear of the Western dmu of the Medway Valley and the wooded slopes of the North Downs has been a much appreciated revelation.

Above: The Derby-Sulzer 1,600hp Type 2s (Class 24) were amongst the first of the Pilot Scheme diesels and although usually associated with the London Midland and Scottish Regions a batch of the earliest ones worked on the Southern before the '33s' appeared. They took over the through Birkenhead train on 15 June 1959 and just over a month later Nos 5001/9 are seen leaving Redhill with the 07.35 Birkenhead to Margate. *Stanley Creer*

Below: But steam had not yet entirely disappeared from this route and almost two years later, on 3 June 1961, 'Schools' No 30937, *Epsom*, is seen entering Tonbridge with the 09.10 Margate to Birkenhead made up of ex-GW stock. Regular through trains to and from the Great Western by way of the Tonbridge-Reading line began as early as 1863 but by the 1960s most passengers found it quicker to travel by way of London and the last through train ran in September 1964. Which was rather a pity as I always enjoyed travelling non-stop between Tonbridge and Redhill in a Swindon-built bow-ender rather than the more usual all stations in a 'birdcage' set or in a narrow-bodied ex-Hastings corridor.

Below: The Redhill-Tonbridge line was once part of the SEC's main line to the Kent Coast and the odd through train continued to use this route until the end of steam. But the South Eastern soon built its own line by way of Orpington and Sevenoaks. On 10 June 1950 almost new 'West Country' Pacific No 34103 *Calstock* in the charge of the up 'Golden Arrow' prepares to tackle the continuous climb from Tonbridge through the North Downs by way of Hildenborough, Sevenoaks and Polhill. *E. R. Wethersett*

Bottom: One of the Wainwright 'H' class 0-4-4Ts, No 31193, pulls out of Tonbridge on 28 March 1959 on its way to take up duties on the Paddock Wood-Maidstone West branch with a two-coach ex-LSW push-pull set whilst sister engine No 31517 creeps into the picture, coming off the shed.

Right: On the same day rebuilt 'Merchant Navy' No 35015, *Rotterdam Lloyd*, speeds through Tonbridge with the down 'Golden Arrow'. The all-Pullman make-up of the early postwar years had by this date proved too optimistic. As in the 1930s a number of ordinary carriages were now incorporated, then because of the economic recession, but in the late 1950s for the quite opposite reason — increasing affluence was attracting more and more Continental travellers to the airlines.

Below right: Rebuilt 'West Country' No 34022, *Exmoor*, slows on the approach to Tonbridge with the up 'Man of Kent' in preparation for the sharp curve at the west end of the station at the end of the long, dead straight racing stretch from Ashford.

Bottom right: Twelve '33/2' diesel-electrics, were designed with specially narrow bodies for the Hastings line. They came out in 1962, all six 'N1s' being withdrawn in November of that year. One of the '33/2s' pulls out of Tonbridge West Yard in 1975 with coal empties. It bears the Hither Green-Hoo Junction headcode, which can hardly be correct, the Hastings one is 4B.

Right: Only a Hastings unit's mother would think its flat slab sides beautiful. Class 203 (6B) No 1033 one of the sets incorporating a now vanished buffet car stands at Hastings ready to depart for Charing Cross on a sunny Saturday evening in the summer of 1969.

Below: The three-cylinder version of the 'N', was the 'N1'. There were only six of them, the last, No 31880 seen here at Tonbridge Shed on 29 September 1956. The 'N1s' were narrower over the cylinders than the 'Ns' and were thus able to work over the Tonbridge-Hastings line.

Bottom: A 6PAN/PUL Victoria-Hastings-Ore express passes St Leonards West Marina in October 1959. The old engine shed, once the home of 'Schools', 'Ls' and 'Terriers', is already abandoned, apart from some coal wagons loath to depart, and was subsequently demolished and replaced by the present demu depot. The West Marina station has also gone although St Leonards West, a few hundred yards away and close to Bopeep junction where the Brighton and South Eastern lines converge, remains.   *D. Stubbs*

Left: 'N' class 2-6-0 No 31410 of Stewarts Lane passes Tonbridge with a down freight. Eastern Section engines were generally kept very clean, but No 31410's immaculate condition is due to her just having emerged from overhaul. The 80 'N' class Moguls, together with the bigger-wheeled 'U' class, were probably the most useful engines the Southern ever possessed. They worked every sort of train all over the Southern system, there being very few lines over which they were not allowed. No 31410 was one of the last batch, hence her sloping-topped tender, and came out of Ashford Works in November 1933. She was withdrawn from Guildford Shed exactly 31 years later.

Below: 9 June 1961, five days before the second stage of the Kent Coast electrification and the virtual elimination of steam from the Eastern Section, 'E1' 4-4-0 No 31507 approaches Tonbridge with the 07.24 London Bridge-Ramsgate. The first three coaches are a set of BR standards, still in red and cream livery. This was the last regular working between London and the Kent Coast by an inside-cylinder 4-4-0 (the last 'Schools' working on the Hastings line was the 07.47 from Sevenoaks, that day in the charge of No 30928, *Stowe*, now preserved on the Bluebell Railway). The Ramsgate train actually started from Holborn Viaduct and was worked up the previous evening from the coast by way of Maidstone East and the West Malling line.

Above: The last day of the Hawkhurst branch, 3 June 1961. 'H' class No 31177 stands at Paddock Wood at the northern end of the branch with the 12.39 train whilst a Hastings line demu (Class 202) passes through on the main line heading for Ashford. No 31177's train is one of the Maunsell push-pull two-coach conversions of 1959/60; standing next to it is an ex-LSW set.

Below: 'Schools' No 30919 *Harrow* pulls the empty stock of the 11.35 from Victoria out of Ramsgate station on the last Saturday of steam, 13 June 1959. All around are 4-CEPs and 4-BEPs ready to take over on the following Monday morning. The old order is represented by Maunsell 2-6-0s, an ex-LSW brake/3rd in departmental service on the far left, and 'D' class 4-4-0 No 31501 with her smokebox open, in use as a stationary boiler. An interesting sight just beyond the LSW carriage was a 'King Arthur' with half her wheels on the sleepers rather than the rails and a gang of railwaymen standing around her scratching their heads. Unfortunately when my camera was spotted I was rapidly shooed away.

Top left: Maunsell Moguls had always been a feature of the Eastern Section summer weekend scene, much more so than on the Western Section which had the 'H15' and 'S15' 4-6-0s. The three-cylinder 6ft 'U1s' had the reputation of being the fastest and most powerful of all the 2-6-0s. There were 21 of them, the first being a 1928 rebuild of *River Frome*, one of Maunsell's ill-fated express 2-6-4Ts of 1925, the remainder coming out from Eastleigh in 1931. No 31904 is seen near Dumpton Park with a down London express. The sixth carriage is a Pullman. The use of such vehicles was a tradition on Kent Coast expresses, one that disappeared, of course, with steam. No 31904 was a Stewarts Lane engine and, like others of her class, often appeared on the heaviest Oxted line passenger trains. The 'U1s' were very much passenger engines, although No 31904 ended her career, in 1962, at Norwood Junction, a purely freight depot. The big flat front of Maunsell's three-cylinder Moguls was not generally considered beautiful but I rather liked them for it and the air of powerful purposefulness it gave them. All three pictures on this page were taken on 13 June 1959, the last day of steam at Ramsgate.

Centre left: 'King Arthur' No 30802, *Sir Durnore*, being oiled before taking out a London train. Beyond are an 'N', two 'Cs' and a 'Schools'. *Sir Durnore* had been built with a small six-wheeled tender to enable him to fit on ex-LBSC turntables. He had been transferred to the Eastern Section after the Brighton line electrification but kept his six-wheel tender until receiving a bogie one from a withdrawn Urie 'Arthur' in the mid-1950s. Once again electrification displaced *Sir Durnore*, this time to Nine Elms, for a brief period before withdrawal in July 1961.

Below: Right until the end SECR-built engines were to be found taking their share of the holiday traffic. 'D1s' and 'E1s' were no great surprise but rather more remarkable was 'H' class 0-4-4T No 31326 dwarfed by the carriages of the 09.18 Margate to Birkenhead as the train approaches Ramsgate. The second carriage is a Great Western 12-wheel dining car.

Left: A Margate-Charing Cross express composed of two 4-CEPs (Class 411/2) approaches Dover Marine beneath the far from white cliffs of Dover in 1970. The train has just left Dover Priory and is not actually going into Marine station but as the signal beneath which it is passing indicates, is going to swing westwards and run along the cliffs, cut through Archcliffe and Shakespeare tunnels to Folkestone and then head inland for Ashford.

Below left: By the late 1970s the 4-CEPs and 4-BEPs were approaching their 20th year. For reasons of finance it had not been possible to replace them and so, perhaps surprisingly, Swindon was allocated the task of rebuilding them. This was a drastic operation, involving replacement, but not new, bogies; interiors gutted, guards'

vans ripped out and resited; new seating, lighting and windows, and a public address system. Work had just started when this picture was taken inside Swindon on 1 May 1979.

Above: Strawberry Hill depot on 3 March 1980 from a train on the Shacklegate junction-Fulwell junction curve. Nearest the camera in the sidings is a recently refurbished Class 411 (former 4-CEP) following delivery from Swindon Works, beyond are two Class 508 units.

Below: 10 January 1980 refurbishing of one of the first units had just been completed and it is seen undergoing various stationary tests at Swindon before being sent back to take up work on the Southern.

Above: Two former SECR 0-4-4Ts from Gillingham Shed at Gravesend Central, 20 June 1952. On the right is 'H' class No 31295 with the 15.14 arrival from the Allhallows branch, and on the left 'R' class No 31658 about to move off to collect the carriages of the 15.32 to Allhallows. The branch, which once terminated at Port Victoria whence a steamer plied briefly to the Continent, remains open for freight. No 31658 was one of the few former LCDR locomotives, introduced by Kirtley in 1891, to survive into BR days. *Brian Morrison*

Below: The impressive new bridge over the River Swale, which links the Isle of Sheppey with the mainland, under construction on 1 May 1959, whilst 'C' class 0-6-0 No 31037 eases her way over the old bridge with a Sheerness-Sittingbourne train. Although the ex-LSW '700' class and the former LBSC 'C2Xs' did a limited amount of passenger work their more numerous SEC-built counterparts were true mixed traffic engines; 109 were built between 1900 and 1908 and 106 of them came to BR in 1948, the most numerous of all pre-Grouping classes on the Southern. Fittingly they were the last SEC-built engines to work on BR, three remaining in departmental service at Ashford Works after steam had disappeared elsewhere on the Eastern Section. One, No 592, is preserved on the Bluebell Railway. *Stanley Creer*

Above: Wareham signalbox. Bob Richards signalman turns the wheel which works the level crossing gates, 1 April 1980. The next day a new bridge replacing the level crossing had made the gates redundant and a short while after the wheel and its connections were removed.

Below: The disused Holton Heath box, between Wareham and Hamworthy junction. Note the original LSWR nameplate.

Below: Horsted Keynes, an LBSCR box, E4 *Birch Grove* alongside.   *Bottom:* Alresford signalbox.

Above: Merstham, an ex-LBSCR signalbox on the main Brighton line.

Below: A typical LSWR-built signalbox at Dunbridge on the Salisbury-Romsey line.

Above: No 30903 *Charterhouse* awaits departure from Charing Cross with a Kent Coast express on 24 March 1951. I never thought the 'Schools' looked quite right in BR black, and the Great Western green applied late in their careers was a distinct improvement. At the far end of Charing Cross bridge *Charterhouse* would have passed the Festival of Britain Exhibition, a marvellous show which extended along the South Bank of the river on either side of the railway. *Brian Morrison*

Below: One of the Southern's boldest experiments was the suburban double-decker, seen here about to make its inaugural public run from Charing Cross on 2 November 1949. Its faults soon became clear but we schoolboys found it vastly more exciting than the usual run of suburban units and made a point of riding on it whenever we could, even if this meant travelling to New Cross rather than to New Cross Gate which was really where we meant to go. The upper deck had a rather claustrophobic air and could get very hot, but that didn't dim its appeal as far as we were concerned, although I can quite see why regular commuters on the Dartford Loop, where it worked all its days, were not so enamoured. *F. G. Reynolds*

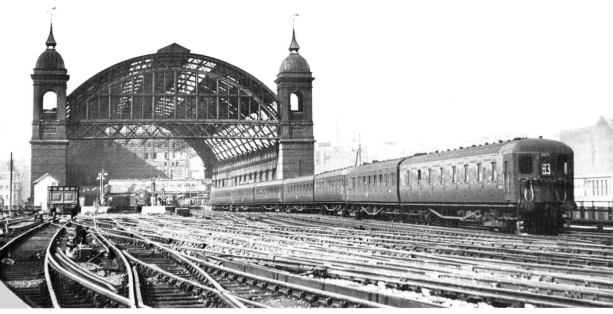

Top: Holborn Viaduct is very much a suburban traffic station, although Continental expresses could once be found within its precincts, and Blackfriars next door possessed that extraordinary collection of engravings of exotic foreign destinations on its masonry. A couple of pre-Grouping 4-SUBs stand in the old station, now completely rebuilt. On the left is an ex-LBSC set on a Catford Loop to Sevenoaks service and on the right an ex-LSW one about to set off on the round-the-houses Wimbledon, Sutton, West Croydon route. This latter journey embraced not only ex-SEC, LBSC and LSW tracks, but also the Southern Railway-built St Helier line. *R. C. Riley*

Above: The 17.07 for Gillingham, composed of four 2-HALs leaves Cannon Street, 6 May 1957. The HALs succeeded the BILs and

clearly showed the hand of Bulleid, who had taken over from Maunsell in 1939. The first batch of 76 came out in July 1939 for the Medway electrification, 16 more appearing after the Reading line was electrified. They were several steps backwards compared with the 2-BILs. The motorcoaches were in all respects except usage purely suburban vehicles with their seven compartments unconnected by corridors and without lavatories. The seats were not very comfortable, the windows except on the corridor side of the trailer composite, were small with unnecessarily large radiussed corners. The 2-HALs remained on their original duties until replaced in 1958 on the Medway lines by 2-HAPs, when they moved over to the Central and Western Sections and worked indiscriminately with the BILs. *Brian Morrison*

Below: Amongst the exhibits in the railway section of the 1951 Festival of Britain was 'Britannia' class Pacific No 70004 *William Shakespeare*, chosen no doubt because of his name. When the Festival was over *William Shakespeare*, along with No 70014, *Iron Duke*, was sent to Stewarts Lane, the only 'Britannias' ever to be permanently allocated to the Southern Region. They were popular, handsome locomotives, and for a number of years *William Shakespeare* was given Stewarts Lane star turn, the 'Golden Arrow' Bearing various embellishments, including the French and English flags, and kept spotless, *William Shakespeare* in charge of his rake of chocolate and cream Pullmans provided a daily spectacle of such splendour as the ensemble swept through East Brixton, Penge, Sydenham Hill and other centres of civilisation unused to unrestrained displays of colour and exuberance that even the least railway minded suburban traveller turned to stare and admire.

Bottom: A picture of No E5011 in charge of the 'Golden Arrow' during its last week of operation. The stationmaster walks up the traditional Continental platform, No 8 to inspect the immaculate locomotive.

Above: An equally glamorous train which managed to survive until 1980 was the 'Night Ferry'. A rake of Wagon-Lits sleepers stirs thoughts of romantic and perhaps dangerous journeys across the Continent in the company of film stars, secret agents, diplomats, refugees and the like. The reality was by no means a let-down. When I worked as a porter at Victoria I often used to carry passengers' luggage into the 'Night Ferry' and the atmosphere in the sleepers with their typical Continental style windows which let right down so you could hand the luggage in, the French attendants and the expectation of going to sleep amongst the Kent hopfields and waking up in the heart of either Paris or Brussels, was something

unique and special. Battle of Britain No 21C156, *Croydon*, with her original number and livery, and an 'L1' 4-4-0 — a common combination — stand ready to depart on 15 December 1948. The second carriage is a Pullman, a very rare sight. Although the 'Night Ferry' always conveyed a number of BR carriages between Dover and Victoria, Pullmans were never part of the normal complement. *British Rail*

Below: Class 71s took over the 'Night Ferry', as they did the 'Golden Arrow'. In 1969 No E5010 stands with her Wagon-Lits beneath the Night Ferry sign at No 2 platform, Victoria. The clock shows almost 11.30, a very late arrival.

Below: For a period in the 1930s and 1940s a number of ex-LSW and LBSC locomotives worked on the Eastern Section from Stewarts Lane, the practice dying out in early BR days with the advent of large numbers of Bulleid light Pacifics. Class T9 4-4-0 No S282 climbs Grosvenor Bank on 30 July 1949 with an eight coach 'long set' of SEC-built 'Birdcage' non-corridors on her way to the Kent coast. *C. C. B. Herbert*

Bottom: The 'Kentish Belle' began life as the 'Thanet Belle', introduced by British Railways in 1948 between Victoria and Ramsgate via the Medway route. It was renamed in 1951 and kept going with its fading if rather splendid wooden-bodied Pullmans until the end of steam on the Kent Coast. No 34017, *Ilfracombe*, is in charge of the up train at Shortlands, 2 August 1954. *Stanley Creer*

Left: Former SEC 4-4-0s were a feature of Kent Coast trains on Summer Saturdays right until the end of steam. Class L No 31780 heads through Bickley on 23 August 1958. The 'Ls' were always known as the 'Germans' for the very good reason that Nos 31772-81 were built by Borsig of Berlin and shipped across a matter of months before the outbreak of World War 1. Nos 31760-71 came from Ashford. Although Wainwright is credited with the design of the 'Ls' they show clearly the hand of Maunsell, who had taken over at Ashford in 1913, and they bore a strong resemblance to Maunsell's rebuilds of Wainwright's 'D' and 'E' classes.

Below: Six weeks earlier on 12 July 1958 the same train was in the charge of No 31497 an E1 class 4-4-0 of Bricklayers Arms shed. Built as an E class in 1907 No 31497 was rebuilt in 1920 and withdrawn in October 1960.

Above: A last look at a rebuilt Wainwright 4-4-0 Class E1 No 31067 stands in the sidings at the north end of Sevenoaks station on the evening of 13 October 1956 with a Tonbridge train. The carriages are a three-coach non-Birdcage ex-SEC set. Eleven out of the 26 Wainwright 'Es' were rebuilt by Maunsell in 1919-20, the result closely resembling the Midland/LMS Fowler '2P'.
No 31067 was a Stewarts Lane engine and frequently worked Continental expresses in the early 1920s before the 'Arthurs' and 'Nelsons' appeared. No 31067 was the last 'E1' in service, being withdrawn in November 1961.

Below: Sevenoaks might be considered an outer suburban station, although the North Downs form a barrier, protecting the countryside around the town from encroachment by the suburbs proper. With its market and the glorious grounds of Knowle Park in its heart Sevenoaks is still very much a country town. Electrification reached the town 50 years ago, although it was to be more than 30 years before it got any further south. A 4-EPB (Class 415/1) stands ready to leave for Charing Cross whilst the old SEC station undergoes a much-needed face-lift, in June 1976.

Top: Unique are the 10 motor luggage vans built in 1959-61 to work with emus and provided with traction batteries so that they can propel themselves over the non-electrified harbour lines at Dover and Folkestone. No 68006 (Class 419) bring up the rear of a boat train speeding through Sevenoaks, June 1976.

Above: The evening sun lights up the 'Golden Arrow' as it heads through Sevenoaks towards the North Downs and Polhill in September 1969. The loading gauge arm has gone although the structure still stands and the yard was still in use in 1980. At this

late stage in the 'Arrow's' career the number of Pullmans had been reduced to three all-metal ones of 1951, repainted in blue and grey livery. They were the final examples of a tradition which began in 1910, or, if one considers the LCDR Wagon-Lits, 1889. Royalty has travelled over Southern rails since the early days of Queen Victoria's reign. She may have preferred the Great Western route to Windsor but she regularly used the LSWR on her way to Osborne House on the Isle of Wight, and both the LSW and the LBSC companies built Royal Trains. The Southern, however, preferred Pullmans, but since 1948 a remarkable variety of coaching stock has been used, ranging from electric multiple-units to the complete British Rail Royal Train.

Left: 'T9s' were often in charge of royalty in the 1920s and 1930s, between Portsmouth and the capital at the beginning or end of tours of the Empire. 4-4-0s continued to perform Royal duties in the 1940s and 1950s, the 'Schools' class being regularly employed on the train of Pullmans which conveyed the Queen and the Duke of Edinburgh to the Derby. On 2 June 1954 No 30936, *Cranleigh*, eases slowly through Reedham station on her way to Tattenham Corner. The train passed through at walking pace in order that children from the nearby orphanage might get a good view of the Queen and Duke.

Above: The return journey that day was from Chessington South. 'West Country' No 34011, *Tavistock*, stands beside the distinctive reinforced concrete awning ready to depart. *Brian Morrison*

Top right: On 11 July 1969 the complete Royal Train with an ex-LNWR clerestory brake/1st of 1905 leading, passes Winfrith Atomic Energy Research Establishment behind a Class 47 on its way with the Queen and the Duke of Edinburgh to Dorchester. *Tony Trood*

Centre right: A spotless Class 47 reverses the new Royal Train — put together for the Silver Jubilee in 1977 — into Branksome sheds, Bournemouth for servicing prior to taking the Queen and the Duke of Edinburgh back to Windsor after visiting Poole and Bournemouth in March 1979.

Bottom right: Victoria, being only a few yards from Buckingham Palace, is a favourite Royal terminus. The replacement of sea travel by air has increased its popularity for almost all foreign visitors now arrive at Gatwick Airport and take the train thence. Unlikely motive power in 1970 for the subsequently deposed and murdered King of Afghanistan was a 'Warship' borrowed from the Western Region. By this date a number of the class was already withdrawn. The train consisted of BR Mk I stock, Metro-Cammell Pullmans of 1960, and one of the massive Gresley East Coast Joint Stock saloons of 1908.

Left: Bluebell beauties: (above left) An immaculate 'C' 0-6-0 No 592 and 'U' 2-6-0 No 1618 combine forces on the 14.50 ex-Sheffield Park, near Freshfield on 14 September 1980. (Left) Back in service again, the preserved 'Q1' 0-6-0 is fittingly harnessed to a train of mostly Bulleid coaches on 5 October 1980.
Brian Stephenson; John Titlow

This page: Never part of the Southern Railway, although later included in the Southern Region was the Kent & East Sussex Railway. Two views of preservation: (above) Rolvenden, looking towards the level crossing, at Easter 1970 with the two 'Terriers' and two ex-USA tanks. (Right) More recently, on 15 April 1979, a Hunslet Austerity tank approaches Rolvenden on a Wittersham Road-Tenderden train.
Arthur E. Loosley; Brian Morrison

This page: Mid-Hants revivals. (Above) 'U' 2-6-0 No 31806, originally built as a 'River' 2-6-4T in 1926, is undergoing restoration at Ropley in October 1980. (Left) Preserved rebuilt Bulleid Light Pacific No 34016 *Bodmin* stands at Ropley on the Mid-Hants Railway on 29 March 1980; following restoration over the previous seven years she is about to embark on her first full season at work.

Right: Southern strangers. Yorkshire seems to be the place to see Southern steam at work today. Two examples are (top right) 'S15' 4-6-0 No 841, now known as *Greene King*, leaving Grosmont with a Pickering train, on the North York Moors Railway on 25 August 1980. (Bottom right) Bulleid light Pacific No 34092 *City of Wells* adds to a fine scene at Oakworth, Keighley & Worth Valley Railway, in August 1980.
Peter Harvis; John Sagar

From an offshore island . . . still on the Southern. (Left) A flashback from preservation to shortly before the end of regular steam operation on the Isle of Wight, with 'O2' 0-4-4T No 16 *Ventnor* at Shanklin in December 1966. (Below) Welcome revival — 'Terrier' 0-6-0T No 8 *Freshwater*, in steam again for the first time for 14 years, on 22 August 1980.
M. Dunnett; Joma Enterprises